From Norman Thomas Remick

For the Personal Collection

of

Joshua Johnson

I know when you read this book, and do what it says to do, you will spring ahead of your fellow students and friends in life.

Best wishes,

Norman Thomas Remick

6/27/'09

GOING BEYOND

LEADERSHIP OF CHARACTER

*

KEYS TO UNLOCKING THE SECRETS OF
HOW TO BE A *GREAT* LEADER

by
NORMAN THOMAS REMICK

Author of:
Mr. Jefferson's Academy: The Real Story
Understanding West Point, Leaders of Character, and Thomas Jefferson

ROVANI - New Jersey
2008

2

All persons in this book are real, unless otherwise indicated. A few of the names have been changed for security reasons or at the request of the individual. No attempt has been made to put the stories in this book in historical chronological order. Rather, they are used where they best represent an example of the particular Rule or technique of leadership. The best examples of how to be a great leader do not lend themselves to the convenience of chronological order.

Library of Congress Control Number: 2008920243

Library of Congress Copyright Registration Number: 07- 000000864

For comments or information contact:

Norman Thomas Remick
P.O. Box 200
Barnegat, N. J. 08005
Fax: 609-698-5117

MANUFACTURED ENTIRELY IN THE UNITED STATES OF AMERICA

CONTENTS

DEDICATION   4

PART I: TAKE CARE OF YOU

Chapter 1: How To Make This Book Work For You   5

PART II: TAKE CARE OF YOUR PEOPLE

Chapter 2: Do This ... And You Can Avoid Trouble   17

Chapter 3: Do This ... And It Will Work Wonders For You   35

Chapter 4: Do This ... It's What Everyone Wants   65

Chapter 5: Do This ... It's An Appeal That Everyone Loves 86

Chapter 6: Do This ... And The Whole World Is With You   117

PART III: TAKE CARE OF DOING IT WELL

Chapter 7: Implementing What You Have Learned   149

ACKNOWLEDGMENT   153

ALSO BY NORMAN THOMAS REMICK   154

DEDICATION

THIS BOOK IS DEDICATED TO WEST POINT AND THE LONG GRAY LINE OF WEST POINTERS WHO HAVE DONE MORE THAN ANY TO BUILD THE AMERICAN NATION, AND WHO NEVER FAILED TO FOLLOW CLOSE ORDER BEHIND THE WEST POINT AND WEST POINT SONS OF AN EARLIER DAY TO BE AMERICA'S LIFEGUARDS AND GLADIATORS AND WAR-GUARDIANS IN THE ARENA OF BATTLE AND RAGING TIDES OF INTERNATIONAL CONFLICT.

IF AMERICA SHOULD LAST A THOUSAND YEARS, PEOPLE WILL LOOK BACK AND SAY, "THIS WAS OUR MOST NOBLE AND HONORABLE INSTITUTION. THERE IS NO OTHER INSTITUTION IN AMERICA FROM WHICH SO FEW HAVE BEEN OWED SO MUCH BY SO MANY."

************* *PART I* *****************

TAKE CARE OF YOU
*

Chapter 1: How To Make This Book Work For You

In 1944, during World War II, my mother awoke one day in Paterson, New Jersey to find that she had become a single parent with three kids to feed and no money. She told me that she cried right in front of the authorities when they said they might have to put me, still a baby, in an orphans' home, and put my older brothers, Conrad and Thomas, in foster homes. My mother, early on, taught me how to pray, and I can actually remember later, as still a little tot, praying to God that they would not put me in an orphans' home. This was such a traumatic experience that it has stuck in my memory all these years.

Mom told me she pleaded with the authorities to not take us away from her, telling them, "I promise that I'll work my fingers to the bone to support my three kids, if you'll just give me a chance." Pinching her pennies, and catching buses, and getting her mother to be with us while she worked were only the tip of the iceberg when it came to the stressful and frightening obstacles she had to overcome. But, she doggedly stuck to her one clear goal to keep her kids!

We were originally from the Depression-ridden coal-mining town of Dickson City, Pennsylvania (a suburb of Scranton). Mom told me we moved to Paterson, New Jersey because it was booming with jobs there during World War II. I remember that Mom did fulfill her promise to the authorities by indeed practically working her fingers to the bone at two jobs she managed to land. She knew both jobs would be very hard work, but they would put bread on the table, and hopefully, keep the authorities from the door.

The first job was at a silk mill in Paterson. The place was a veritable sweatshop situated at the foot of Paterson's famous

Great Falls, the national historic monument originally founded in 1791 by Alexander Hamilton during our nation's infancy. Each day she had to wash the few pieces of clothing that she had to her name because they ended up completely soaked with sweat after her rushing from loom to loom all day for eight hours in that factory's unbelievable heat and humidity. She then had to rush like heck to catch the two buses needed to get to her second job at a World War II "defense plant" on Main Street in Clifton, New Jersey. There, she told me, she worked in the electro-plating department, anodizing and plating parts that went into America's war machines. She had to wear coveralls and rubber galoshes so she could slosh back and forth across the wet and puddled floors while lugging 20 pound plating barrels and plating fixtures in and out of 50 gallon acid tanks, water rinse tanks, and plating baths.

Mom earned her wings in the eyes of the authorities. They never again came knocking at our door. And, although both of those jobs were backbreaking work, the heat of her burning desire and her dogged determination to achieve her one clear goal -- keep her kids -- melted away the aches and pains, and kept her eyes on the prize. Today when I think of it, I'm so proud of her it makes me want to cry.

Why the "This is Your Life" story? It's to show you that, if you have the burning desire and dogged determination, you can overcome most obstacles and achieve any goal. With the almost magical character traits of desire, determination, and hard work, you can do wonders. The fact that you have begun to read this book is proof that you do have the desire to rise and soar like an eagle above the maddening crowd of leaders to become, not just an ordinary leader or leader of character, but a rare bird -- a great leader of character in real life. But, do not for one single minute think you can do that by simply flipping through these pages. This is not just a book for reading. It's a book for action.

Thomas Jefferson said that the greatest aim of education is not merely acquiring culture and knowledge, but turning that culture and knowledge into practical action. That's what this book does. It gives you knowledge on the fine art of leadership, and then helps you to turn that knowledge into a special kind of practical action that will make you a great real-life leader of character. You will discover that this book is a working handbook for great real-life leaders of character.

Do you know what Julius Caesar did in the year 54 BC after he successfully negotiated the turbulent waters of the English Channel in small wooden ships and landed his mighty Roman Legions on the shores below Britain's white cliffs of Dover? He proceeded to lead his army up to the top of those chalky white cliffs, march them over to the edge, and make them look down below where they could see the yellow, orange, and red plumes of the fires (that he had some of his men intentionally set) that were slowly devouring all of their wooden ships. That was how Caesar made certain that the men in his army would internalize the desire and determination to strictly go forward to achieve the goal. He removed all of their lingering thoughts that it was possible to retreat to the past. He burned their bridges -- in this case, their ships -- behind them. There was but one thing left for them to do: strengthen their bodies; pump up their hearts; readjust their minds; march forward; survive off the land; conquer and master the Britons. And history shows, that's just what they did.

That was the Julius Caesar way of leadership: burn your bridges behind you so you can put your whole mind and your whole heart into going forward. And that's exactly what I'm telling you to do. Set aside your old ways of thinking about leadership. Burn those old bridges behind you. Pump up your heart. Re-adjust your mind. March forward to conquer and master the techniques that I give you in this book.

As a pilot, I love to take what is actually just a useless assemblage of metal and plastic and nuts and bolts when it is sitting motionless on the ground, and move it forward down the runway until it overcomes the pull of gravity and lifts off the ground into the air. It then becomes a magnificent, useful, fine-tuned machine called an airplane. It is now capable of taking you to Disneyland in Florida, if you want it to, as long as it keeps moving forward. If it stops moving forward, however, it will sink back down to mother earth where you began.

Likewise, you are the pilot of your destination, your future. This book is your "airplane", also an assemblage of the basic "nuts and bolts" -- the basic techniques -- that you need to reach your destination, your goal of becoming one of those rare birds -- a great real-life leader. But, like our airplane, this book is just a useless assemblage of those "nuts and bolts" unless you start moving forward by putting its basic techniques into practical action as soon as you read about them. If you fail to do that, you will never overcome life's pull of gravity that keeps you on the ground with every Tom, Dick, and Harry who calls himself a leader. If you start to take positive action, however, you will move forward and begin rising above the Toms, Dicks, and Harrys, who are leaders-in-name only, to new heights of great real-life leadership ability. You will not sink back down to mother earth where you began. And please know and always remember this: when you put the wrench to the nuts and bolts of great real-life leadership, put your whole heart into it. That is so important.

Speaking of putting your whole heart into it, I'll never forget the first time one Sunday morning that I attended a Mass given by the Reverend John Wightman of St. Mary's R.C. Church in Manahawkin, New Jersey. The then eighty-six year old priest, one of only three remaining out of his Seminary class of twenty that was ordained in the diocese of Newark, had been retired for several years and wanted to find an arrangement in which he could resume celebrating mass. But, he could not handle more than one mass a week at his age. Reverend Ken Tuzeneu, pastor of St. Mary's, showing his kindness and empathy, found a way to help him out, telling him he could immediately offer him the early, always half empty 7:30 mass on Sunday mornings in the parish center. Father Wightman told us his immediate response was a quick and simple, "I'll take it."

I happened upon the 7:30 Mass that morning because I was scheduled to do a book signing that afternoon at West Point, a 2 hour drive away. When they finished the Scripture readings from Deuteronomy and Corinthians about people not living on bread alone, and the Gospel according to John about Jesus and eternal life, it then came time for Father Wightman to deliver his Homily. Everyone expected him to get right into speaking from prepared notes on the usual Catholic doctrine regarding the readings. But he didn't. Far from it. Instead he casually talked with us, as if in a one to one conversation, and gave us an inspiring, convincing, down to earth revelation of how he was, long ago, called to God, and offered a logical explanation of who we are, why God put us here on this planet, and where we are going. When he finished, the whole place was dead silent. We were all just blown away by the renewed faith and enlightenment that father Wightman had instilled in our hearts and minds.

What was the secret behind his moving inspiration? He simply drew from deep down upon his heartfelt, lifelong, divinely inspired inner feelings of purity and certainty. Did he preach? No. Did he teach? Yes. He explained, and put his whole heart into it.

From that day forward, I enthusiastically attended the good Father Wightman's masses, and awoke early every Sunday morning to do so, even after staying up late on Saturday nights to watch "Leno" or an old John Wayne movie. So did lots of other people. The 7:30 a.m. Mass went from half empty to full.

The point is, however you choose to put the techniques that you learn in this book into action, remember this: put your whole heart into it, because what comes from the heart gets into the hearts of others. If you do that, you will become someone who is not just a boss, or even a boss-with-character, or leader-in-name-only, but someone who is at the leading edge of your generation.

You are probably asking yourself, "What is actually meant by a leader of character?" And, "What is this boss-with-character or leader-in-name-only vs. great real-life leader of character dichotomy?" They are two fair questions. Let me give you a quick tutorial on the subject from my book, *Understanding West*

Point, Leaders of Character, and Thomas Jefferson, to answer those questions.

"Leader of character" has become a common "term of art" that is associated with the world's premier academic-leadership teaching college, West Point. But, in truth, it is much more than just a term of art. A person who has character is someone who has captured that rare personal quality called Virtue. Now you must be asking, "What exactly is Virtue?" So before we go on, I'll try to clear that up for you, too.

The word, Virtue (that you often hear being casually bandied about) describes eternal, unchanging, absolute "Ideals" having to do with right and wrong, good and evil. And did you know that Virtue actually has three branches: morals, ethics, and character? I'll explain.

Morals, as in moral virtues, also sometimes called moral traits, deals with your relation to God and to absolute things like un-redefinable truth, duty, trust, honor, honesty, etc. Lying, cheating, stealing, lusting, and so on, are their opposites.

Ethics, as in ethical virtues, or ethical traits, deals with you and society. They are things like justice, freedom, and fairness.

Character, as in character virtues, or character traits, deals with you personally. It is things like desire, courage, loyalty, discipline, determination, and responsibility.

When West Point uses the phrase "leaders of character", that phrase really means "leaders of Virtue" -- leaders having morals, ethics, and character, not just having character.

Thomas Jefferson believed that people are born with an innate sense of the virtues, yes, an innate sense of morals, ethics, and character. He preached that your strength of virtues, like the strength of your arms or legs, can be maintained through training and daily practice. West Point still follows that philosophy. West Point cadets are required to practice all of the virtues, every day. And there is no reason why <u>you</u> cannot also practice the virtues every day on your own, if you have the desire and determination.

Now for the second question: What is the difference between boss-with-character, or leader-in-name-only of character, and great real-life leader of character? It is the difference between a real leader, and someone who is merely put in charge and given the title, "leader", by fiat. For example, I have known people who are in the ranks who are of high character, but who have remained in the ranks, simply because they did not have the ability to get things done well. They did not learn what you are learning in this book -- the way to win your followers, or your superiors, or anyone else, over to your side.

Folks who are the boss can make their people jump through hoops or get them coffee from the cafeteria, because their people don't want to get fired. And, it takes no talent to make people give you a snappy salute, out of respect for your rank but not necessarily out of respect for you, if you are a military officer who is in command of those people. But, there is only one way on this God's green earth that you can get people to put forth their Sunday-best behavior and effort to do the very best they can do for you. And there is only one way to get followers, or superiors, or anyone else to do it your way. You have to learn the secret of getting them to want to do the very best they can do, or want to do it your way, willingly and voluntarily. And that is precisely the secret you are reading this book to learn, and will learn.

Some people are born with charisma, but there are no such animals in captivity as people who are born as great leaders of character. So, I repeat. Whether in charge of Strykers or plows, of assembly lines or word processors, the difference between bosses or even bosses-with-character and great real-life leaders of character is this: great real-life leaders of character have the ability to get things done, and the ability to get people to do their very best by getting them to want to do their very best, willingly and voluntarily. And, if you've ever led people, you know that this is a formidable challenge.

By now, a lot of readers are probably saying, "I don't need this kind of training. I've been into leadership for so long now, I certainly know it all, if anyone does." That's fair enough. I remember feeling that same way myself a number of years ago.

I have a library of hundreds of books that I have read on management and leadership and history and philosophy and psychology and the lives of great leaders. But, as the years went by, I gradually came to realize that bosses, or even bosses-with-character, are horses of a different color than what I am calling great real-life leaders of character. Being a great real-life leader of character is an art. And like all art, it requires but a few principles -- in this case: morals, ethics, and character -- and a whole lot of practical techniques. When I think back over the years, I am astonished at how woefully in need I often was of this art myself, and how little I actually understood it, despite all of my reading, education, and experience.

For example, I wish I could have put my hands on a book like the one you are reading when, in 1973, because of my work, I had to turn my back on the world I knew and go off to "merry old England" with my wife Diane, and my eighteen month old son Kyle, to implant a new company in the microwave semiconductor industry of Europe that would be entirely my own. What a huge challenge it was. I was not acting on behalf of some major American corporation, as is typically the case in England. I had to set up a bona-fide company completely on my own with no outside help, and do it from scratch. I knew it would be tough, but I had no choice.

The folks at the British Registry of Companies looked at me with big question marks on their faces and asked me, "Why is it you are the only one we have ever seen who is trying to do this on your own account, as a lone wolf?" It was a challenge to answer them and to convince them, as well as the British Home Office, and MI-5, and other British organizations, and their counterparts throughout Europe, that I was simply and absolutely doing what I alleged I was doing. For remember this, the Vietnam War may have been winding down, but the Cold War was still raging and ratcheting up.

It was not only a challenge, but it was stressful and worrisome to have to lead a triple life as: first and foremost (to me, anyway) an American dad and husband at "home" in England with family; second, a "British" engineer, industrialist, and company

CEO producing bona fide, saleable microwave components at a bona fide factory in England; and third, when traveling throughout Europe, being my own special "intelligence service." I was establishing and cultivating contacts, marketing my products, and sniffing-out the latest sophisticated, state of the art technology on the drawing boards, always bucking up against clandestine operatives doing the same thing in a Europe of multiple languages and Cold War intrigues. But, you're not going to believe me when I tell you what was my biggest challenge, once I got a handle on those other stresses, worries, and challenges of making my "credentials" believable. It was leadership, pure and simple. It was figuring out how to get the people who worked on the shop floor in my factory to want to cooperate, want to do their best work, want to follow me, and thus, make my work -- my mission -- and my family's life in England a success.

When I first started my company, "Packages For Semiconductors", my employee-worker relationships were as cold and damp and foggy as a January morning in London. It's not that my staff in England disliked me. We basically got along okay. In fact, they said that their only knock on me, like the British knock on all of their "American cousins" in England since the time of the Second World War, was that I was overfed, overpaid, oversexed, and over there. None of that was actually true of me, except of course, being over there.

My first instinct was to put our "British cousins" in their place. But, I said to myself: "Remick, any fool who is the boss can do that, and I think I can do better than be a fool". So, I resolved with a burning desire and dogged determination to change their cool attitudes toward me into warmth and cooperation. I decided to look at it like the challenge of a sport. But this wasn't all fun. It was a sport in which I had to come up a winner in the end, or I would be in deep "doo-doo".

I figured that every college on either side of the Atlantic would have a practical working manual to help me. After all, Rockefeller and Carnegie and Chrysler and General Electric had paid people like Lee Iacocca and Jack Welch tens of millions of dollars a year, not because they were super smart, and not because they knew more about automobiles or engineering than anyone else. As a matter of fact, Iacocca and Welch both said in books they wrote that most people working for them knew a lot more than they did. They were paid their millions because of their human relations ability to get things done, and done well. Then wouldn't you think there would be books and courses all over the place to teach the highest-paid abilities in the world?

So I thought I would have no difficulty whatsoever with finding a practical working manual to use as a guidebook. When I looked around for one, however, there was none. It became obvious to me that I would have to develop my own techniques in order to turn my workers' attitudes around. So I got down to work with a burning desire and dogged determination to prove the old saying, "It's difficult to make a friend of an Englishman, but once you do, you have a friend for life."

I read the life stories of great leaders, from Jesus of Nazareth to the modern Popes, from Alexander the Great to General Douglas MacArthur, from Socrates to Thomas Jefferson, jotting down notes like I was working on a doctorate degree. I drew from my leadership readings, from my own personal experiences, and from the experiences of other people. Being no genius at this, it took me a year to figure it all out, but I finally got it. I finally got the knack. I developed my own practical ideas and techniques. I became an expert at this new and different kind of sport. I felt I had a winning game plan.

As I began to put my whole heart into turning my ideas, and techniques, and game-plan into practical action, I learned that I could turn my employees' attitudes around the same way that I had learned how to fly an airplane and ski down a mountain: by sincerely and bull-headedly trying it over and over again until I succeeded. Once I got it right, my employees' attitudes began to change very sharply.

My key people, Maureen Hewitt and Mike Hewitt, went from being supervisor and works manager to becoming lifelong friends with whom we shared the happy times of parties and weddings, and the sadness of funerals. Our administrative assistant, Irene Seders, became a friend who accompanied us on trips to places from Lands End in the southwest of England to Edinburgh up north in Scotland, during which she willingly filled-in for us as "nanny" to our young son Kyle. Over the years, hundreds of employees who started out cool and indifferent became warm and friendly neighbors. When the trade union organizer came to my factory, my employees overwhelmingly voted to turn him away by a vote of more than 50 to one.

So, you might say, I began to write this book decades ago. It did not come strictly out of the "leadership laboratory" which is West Point, or out of the libraries at Rutgers, West Point, or Cambridge in England, though I certainly did read enough to do a Ph.D. on the subject. It came out of something far more important -- the "leadership laboratory of real life."

When I do book signings, for example, I always personalize my books by speaking with each person for several minutes and by writing a short note to them. When the opportunity presents itself, I always talk at length with people to hear their stories. And, back years ago, as a graduate instructor in a human relations course, I heard many, many wondrous life experiences of students from every living generation and every age group. In short, I've spoken to thousands of people and heard thousands of stories that come from the laboratory of real life.

This book is the distillation of a lifetime of the practical leadership techniques that grew and evolved out of thirty years of my management and leadership gigs here in the USA and at my successful company in England. It is the extract of thirty years of study and observation and trial-and-error that was a part of my life and heart and mind during all of those years. And, as I have said, this book draws water from the well of other people's successful experiences and challenges, and the inspirational stories of some of the greatest leaders of all time whom I have read about in history. In short, you might say that the stories I tell you are gold that is mined from my own mined and coined at my own mint. This book weighs only several ounces, but my notes for it weigh in excess of twenty pounds.

I have seen the practical techniques that you will learn in this book literally change the lives of people. I know that sounds more like magic than like leadership. And I know this may sound somewhat hokey to you, but these techniques <u>do</u> work like magic!

With that you are probably wondering: "Does this guy have the monumental chutzpah to tell me this one book of his has the "magic" to take me from being an ordinary, cookie-cutter leader-by-fiat to being a <u>great</u> <u>real-life</u> leader, one who people will actually <u>want</u> to follow, <u>willingly</u>? Well. Yes. That's exactly what I'm telling you. Like any magic trick, it is not very difficult when you learn the secret of <u>what</u> to do, and then learn <u>how</u> to do it. This book is different from all the others because it teaches you <u>both</u> of those things. But let me repeat. I am not handing you a big bag of tricks or a magic wand here to fool people. My book teaches you certain rules and techniques that will only work if they come from your heart.

But, that's enough of this. You picked up this book because you are looking for action. Now it's time to put your whole heart into going forward with a burning desire and dogged determination to make yourself into one of those rare birds -- a <u>great</u> <u>real-life</u> leader of character. Are you ready? Okay then. Let's learn how to work some "magic."

***************** *PART II* *****************

TAKE CARE OF YOUR PEOPLE
*

Chapter 2: Do This ... And You Can Avoid Trouble

Back in 1951, a near-tragic incident occurred at a school in the Northeast part of the United States. It happened during the school's traditional beginning of year convocation when all of the instructors get up on a stage one at a time to describe and "sell" their courses to the young and eager students. One of the instructors was newly hired Gerhardt Heinrich for a psychology course.

Years before that, Gerhardt Heinrich had arrived in America as a youngster with his parents, penniless immigrants from Germany. Five years later, he became a US citizen.

When the USA entered World War II, he volunteered for the Army where he served as an interpreter with US Army intelligence because he spoke German with no English accent. After the war, he entered college on the GI Bill, finished college, and landed the job as psychology instructor at this school in the Northeast USA. He beat out other applicants for the job because he had the unique psychological experience of being a member of the US Army that was fighting against the country of his birth, Germany.

During the days leading up to the big convocation, Gerhardt Heinrich was dripping with confidence. He felt absolutely sure that he could get up on stage, pitch his psychology course, and get a lot of students to sign up for it, even though he was still somewhat self-conscious about his German accent.

Then the day of the convocation arrived. As Gerhardt sat and waited his turn, a paralyzing nervousness began to overtake his mind. Finally, it was his turn to get up and make his pitch. When he stood on the small makeshift stage and faced the large audience, he became terrified. He suddenly realized he could not put his thoughts together intelligently. He froze. To cover up his fear, he tried to look cool and collected by taking a few gingerly steps backward, as if in contemplation. When he tried to start over, he choked. Confused, he backed up by a few more steps, still trying to appear unruffled.

The audience was now dead silent. You could hear a pin drop. He was all alone up there. Like Peter Sellers in the Pink Panther movies, he now tried the old casually-reach-in-your-pocket ploy, pretending that his breakfast receipt was his prepared crib sheet. After fumbling around with the slip of paper for several seconds, trying to gain a little time to compose himself, he started over. Again, his mind drew a blank. He continued fumbling around and becoming more bewildered, but he still managed to keep up the charade, putting on a coy little Inspector Clouseau-like deceptive smile, as if nothing was wrong. Can you picture that? And again, he tried to appear cool by backing up a few more steps. This time, however, that coy little smile on his face abruptly changed into a look of horror. When he took one last step backwards, his foot found nothing below it! He clumsily tumbled off the back end of the stage. With eyeballs popping out, mouth wide-open, arms flailing all over the place, and paper flying in the air, he disappeared from sight!

The order and politeness displayed by the young students in the audience throughout the day suddenly collapsed into a fit of laughter. But that changed just as suddenly into "oos" and "ohs" of concern.

As Gerhardt pulled himself back up onto the two-foot high stage, he was sporting a big friendly smile on his face. Seeing that, everyone broke into spontaneous applause. The prim and proper Mrs. Evans, the moderator of the convocation, stepped forward and said: "Rest assured, students, our Mr. Heinrich has survived a lot worse than this during the recent War".

Now trying to help him, she went on to ask the audience, "In the true spirit of the course he is teaching, wouldn't you all like to hear Mr. Heinrich tell us a little something about how he felt, psychologically, when he was opposing the country in which he was born?" There was again spontaneous applause of approval.

And Gerhard liked the idea, too. For that he felt he needed no preparation. He felt rescued by Mrs. Evans. But was he? We shall see. Read on.

With that big friendly smile on his face, Gerhardt Heinrich once again stepped up to the front of the stage. He marveled to himself at how the students had reverted back to their former quiet, patient, polite behavior. So what automatically rolled off his lips were sincere words of thanks for their concern over him and a sincere compliment on their maturity and patience during the many long hours of the convocation.

He then went on to quip that he had made softer landings falling backwards out of the parachutist jump bay of a B-17 airplane from 10,000 feet high than his horrible exhibit moments ago from 2 feet high. "Ahnd speaking uf ten tausand feet," he said, "Zat reminds me uf za time ve ver attacked by Cherman Luftvaffe airplanes, ahnd ve had to bail out uf our B-17 from ten tausand feet high. It vas during a zecret mission, flying ofer Frahnce. I vas looking out uf za vindow ven I zee dis 'fokker' abuff us" (Imagine how that sounded to a bunch of young girls and boys!). With that, a few subdued giggles could be heard from the girls in the audience. Now try to picture this.

Gerhardt continues, "Ve kept looking, and sure enough, zer he vas, coming in on our tail, shooting at us. Our tailgunner vas shooting back. Zen, I look out, and zer vas anozer 'fokker' coming in from za left zide." A few more students, especially girls, now chime-in with some more subdued giggles.

"Zen anuzer 'fokker' comes difing down on us from abuff." More of the young girls now join-in with less subdued and more contagious giggles.

"All uf a zudden airplanes are zwarming all offer us like a nest uf wasps. It zeemed like efry 'fokker' in za whole damn Luftvaffe vas ahfter us." With that, everyone in the audience begins to chuckle, including the faculty, and some of the girls now begin to uncontrollably laugh out loud with their hands over their mouths trying to hide it.

That brings the proper Mrs. Evans to her feet again to interrupt Gerhardt Heinrich. She steps forward and says, "Quiet-down students. Quiet girls. Let me explain. "Fokker, spelled F-O-K-K-E-R, is a famous name in aircraft in Germany, as Mr. Heinrich will attest. Isn't that so, Mr. Heinrich?"

With that, Gerhardt Heinrich steps forward, and, with his mouth so close to the microphone that his words blast out very loud, he says, "Yah. Dat is so. Howefer, <u>DEES</u> 'FOKKERS' VER MESSERSCHMIDTS!"

There were about three seconds of stunned silence. Then the entire auditorium went ballistic! Everyone howled out loud with so much laughter that they had to hold their stomachs, doubling up in pain. Some were actually rolling in the aisles with convulsions. The once proper young girls were now screaming out loud with laughter. The whole place was out of control, so Mrs. Evans politely dismissed Mr. Heinrich, who was thankful to be able to retreat from the stage.

When the convocation ended, would you believe it? The students were lined up all the way out the door and into the lobby to sign up for Gerhardt Heinrich's course. Imagine that! Psychology. A course that never-before even came close to being filled, now had a waiting list. At any rate, I am told that people continued to tell that story at the school for many years to come, and some people even made a little riddle out of whether the incident was, or was not, an intentional performance by Gerhardt Heinrich.

Here's another little riddle. Why am I telling you this story about the near disastrous teaching debut of a German-born American in a book on leadership? And how does this all apply to you? Can you guess the answer?

If you say it's to show that people can often face death or hardships bravely, and yet let something small like speaking in public shake them up, well, that's certainly a good lesson to take away from this story. However, it's not the answer I'm looking for. Here is the answer: I told you this story because it shows that, in getting people to <u>want</u> to follow you or cooperate with you <u>willingly</u> and <u>voluntarily</u>, it's important to first get those people thinking like they are on your side. And that is our first key to becoming a great leader of character:

KEY # 1: BEGIN BY GETTING PEOPLE ON YOUR SIDE.

Gerhardt Heinrich had astonishing success with getting students to sign up for his psychology course because his fortuitous little "performance" did get them on his side to begin with. But how do you get people on your side without first having to fall off the back of a stage, or something like that? Here's the first of five ways to do it:

1.) - PREPARE.

You should not begin by winging it like Gerhardt Heinrich did. He had a near disaster because he was not prepared. The day was saved only because of his story about being in that B-17 during World War Two. It was a story that he was eminently prepared to tell because it was about his own unique background and life experience. And don't you think it would have been even better -- with less risk of getting fired right on the spot -- if he had prepared ahead of time?

By, PREPARE, do I mean that you should memorize something word for word and give people a speech or lecture on it? Emphatically, not! Why not? Because, when you do that, you are not putting your whole heart into it. You are merely putting your memory into it.

Here's how you should PREPARE. Assemble your thoughts ahead of time. Mine a "gold nugget" from your gold mine of experiences, background, upbringing, or studies. That's worth repeating. Mine a gold nugget from your own gold mine of experiences, background, upbringing, or studies. Sincerely tell your listeners about something in your life that has taught you a lifetime lesson. If you do that, you will gain dedicated listeners, be they those you lead, or those you want to impress. If you do that, I can tell you this. I will also be a dedicated listener.

There are always two sides to every case. But, there are actually <u>three</u> sides to the case of being prepared: first, <u>you</u>; second, <u>your message</u>; third, <u>your listeners</u>. Looking at the <u>you</u> part, you should be like a combination of teacher, evangelist, and missionary trying to convert people to a cause. Next, it will help you to display the qualities of teacher, evangelist, and missionary if you make sure the nugget that you pluck from your own gold mine, the <u>message</u> part, is something that is important to you. But, even more critical, it should be something that is important and interesting to other people, the <u>listener</u> part, as well. Every great leader of character throughout history, from Sparta's Lycurgus to our own Abraham Lincoln, has displayed the qualities of a teacher, evangelist, and missionary. Whether you succeed or not at being a great leader of character -- getting other people to <u>want</u> to cooperate with you <u>willingly</u> and <u>voluntarily</u> -- will, after all is said and done, be entirely determined in the hearts and minds of those other people, not in yours.

Here's another riddle for you. What is:

A pleasure to those who receive it, as well as, a pleasure to those who give it;

Completely free, but worth so much, and costs you nothing to do it;

Something even the rich cannot do without, and, rich and poor equally enjoy;

One of the roots of a happy home, and a way to promote goodwill in business;

A relief valve for those under pressure, and comfort to those who are sad;

Something that lasts but seconds, yet its memory may last forever;

Wonderful to give to someone, who is too tired to give it to you;

And, something that says much more than "I like you", without saying a single word?

I'm talking about a <u>smile</u>. When Gerhardt Heinrich pulled himself up onto the stage once again after clumsily falling off a few minutes earlier, he had a big smile on his face. In spite of the laughter directed at him, his smile spoke volumes to the audience. It said, "I like you." You can bet that made the audience like him, too. You can bet it helped get them on his side. So, here is the second way you can <u>BEGIN BY GETTING PEOPLE ON YOUR SIDE</u>. It's very simple. Just:

2.) – SMILE

I'm not talking about a big, wide, phony put-on smile that any ten year old kid can see through and know is not sincere. I'm talking about a smile that sincerely says, "I'm on your side"; a real smile that comes from deep down within you. There is one exception, however. If you are a military academy cadet, or a new military recruit, for heavens sake, <u>do not</u> begin with a smile!

When Gerhardt Heinrich began speaking again after falling off the stage, the first words that popped into his mind and rolled off his lips were praises and compliments to the young students in the audience for how mature they were in being patient and polite during the entire day. His sincerity radiated to them when he told them he was deeply touched by how quickly their laughter had turned into silence and concern for his well-being. They applauded that too. So the third way you can <u>BEGIN BY GETTING PEOPLE ON YOUR SIDE</u> is:

3.) – GIVE PRAISE AND COMPLIMENTS

Like a smile, giving praise or paying a compliment costs nothing, yet wins an awful lot of goodwill with people for you, be they mayors or mailmen, bosses or bankers. But I'm not talking about phony flattery -- it must be sincere.

Sometimes there positively is some sort of magic when you give someone sincere praise or pay a sincere compliment. As an illustration, I'm going to tell you about a personal experience of mine, which taught me that lasting lifetime lesson.

In 1977, my company in England (that I founded), Packages For Semiconductors, landed a highly coveted trial order for producing microwave diode components that go into the electronics of a combat aircraft for which Plessey Company in England was doing the avionics systems. In order to beat out my Japanese competitor, I would have to make a one-shot, all-or-nothing delivery of the order on or before a certain date, time being of the essence. That meant, if we failed to deliver the complete trial order on time, we would get the ax. My Japanese competitor would win the order.

All the parts that go into producing the microwave diode component were coming together nicely when, late one evening, at a very odd time for England, the telephone in my office began to ring off the hook. I finally decided to pick it up. It was the supplier from Connecticut who makes the last piece we were waiting for, a tiny threaded copper heat sink that is an important part of my diode component. He flat-out declared that he could not deliver the parts on time. What! That meant our contract would be cancelled! All of our labor, material, and overhead costs may as well be flushed down the toilet bowl. Goodwill that took years to establish with Plessey and the Ministry of Defense might be history. And all because of one little screw machine shop – one man?

All of my phone calls to Connecticut failed to get a rise out of anyone. That's when I thought of what Abraham Lincoln had said under such predicaments, "When all else fails, take a walk to the woodshed and get a big stick." So, I decided to travel to Waterbury, Connecticut in person to see the owner of the screw-machine shop, Jack McHugh, at what by now I had visualized in my mind as being his little house of horrors.

When I drove up to the address I had written down, I thought it surely must be incorrect. It was one of those large, old, three-story, red brick factories, not the small screw-machine shop I was looking for. Just as I was kind of chastising myself with, "how the heck did I get the wrong address", I took the trouble to look up (after irate cars passed with horns honking at me), and there it was, right before my eyes, the name of Jack McHugh's company: "ROYAL SCREW CO."

Finally, I was confronting the owner-president, Jack McHugh, in person. The first words that, strangely enough, sincerely and automatically rolled off my lips were, "This is quite an impressive operation you have here, Jack." As his eyes brightened, he replied, "I've devoted my entire adult life trying to make this business into something. Let me take you on the nickel tour."

I could see that Jack was a good guy. I said to myself, "How in the world will I ever be able to get myself to hammer Jack McHugh on delivery?"

During the plant tour, we traded little horror stories about the hard times we each endured starting our companies. His eyes brightened once again, as I told him that he should be proud to be one of the few companies that can successfully screw machine the pure, soft, high conductivity copper that is needed for microwave components, while other companies are only capable of machining lower quality tellurium copper. That, after all, is the reason I placed my order with him. Up to that point, not a word had been said, however, about the basic problem that I came all that way to hammer him on: his inability to deliver my order.

When we finished the plant tour, we took a little break to freshen-up a bit and then met in owner-president Jack McHugh's office. As his secretary poured our coffee, I said to him, "It's time to talk turkey, Jack. Let's get down to business." With that, he interrupted me and said, "I expected you, and our meeting, to be a lot less cordial than this, Norm. And to tell you the truth, I couldn't really blame you if it was. While we were going through the plant, I was running some things through my mind. That's when I decided to pull out all the stops and do whatever I have to do in order to make your parts right now, even if I have to roll up my sleeves and set the machines up myself. When you leave here, you can go away with my personal promise and absolute assurance that your entire order will be delivered to you on time."

Jack McHugh kept his promise. I received my entire order on time. We completed the contract with Plessey on time and beat-out the Japanese competitor. I never had to hammer him, or pay him a premium price, or try to threaten him with anything. What a turn of events! Giving him praise, and sincerely paying him those deserved compliments without ever discussing the problem that triggered my personal visit, had worked some kind of magic that got him on my side and got him to go out of his way to help me.

The great industrial tycoon, Andrew Carnegie, always said that he had never met a guy doing any job in life who would not practically work until he dropped so as to do the best job that he could do if he knew there were praises and compliments in store for him at the end of the rainbow. Even upon death, Carnegie praised and complimented people. The inscription he had arranged to put on his gravestone read: "Here lies one who knew how to get men around him who were more clever than himself." Isn't that something?

Back in 1830, a young man, who was serving as an enlisted man in the US Army, getting no praise or compliments, decided the life of an officer was more down his alley, and managed to get an appointment to the U. S. Military Academy at West Point. While a cadet, this young man wrote a book of poems that came to the attention of Colonel Sylvanus Thayer, the Superintendent of West Point. Thayer proceeded to GIVE PRAISE AND COMPLIMENTS to the cadet on how professional his work was, and helped him to publish his book, *Poems*. The young cadet was so encouraged by Sylvanus Thayer's praise and compliments that he decided to leave West Point and pursue the life of a writer. West Point's loss was the world's gain, for that ex-cadet went on to have many famous books published. You may have heard of him. His name is Edgar Allan Poe.

So, I shall repeat. It is important to BEGIN BY GETTING PEOPLE ON YOUR SIDE. And to do that, let me tell you, avoid at all costs looking at the bad things or the darker side of people. Start by looking for good things on the brighter side of people so you can find something on which to GIVE PRAISE AND COMPLIMENTS.

When Gerhardt Heinrich crawled back up onto the stage and began to speak, do you remember what else he said? He told the audience he has made better landings falling from a plane at "ten tausend" feet than his horrible exhibit moments ago from two feet. He showed a little humility by playing himself down. His listeners loved it. That, then, is the fourth way in which you can BEGIN BY GETTING PEOPLE ON YOUR SIDE:

4.) - PLAY YOURSELF DOWN.

Do you know what was one of the secrets of President Ronald Reagan's astonishing popularity and great leadership of character? It was his ability to get people on his side to begin with by being humble enough to play himself down. For example, when his critics, mostly the press, accused him of being too old and somewhat lazy, Peggy Noonan in her great book on Reagan, *When Character Was King*, tells us that he would say, "I know hard work never killed anyone, but I figure, why take a chance?" And she says that, on another such occasion, he got reporters on his side to begin with by saying, "I've laid down the law to my staff -- about anything important that happens: No matter what time it is, wake me -- even if I'm in the middle of a cabinet meeting." When reporters got on him about whether he was working hard enough, President Reagan told them, "lately I've been really burning-up the midday oil."

At President Reagan's first State of the Union address, he told the audience, "I am giving this address because George Washington said that all Presidents should report directly to the people." He then turned toward the press, who had been calling him too old, and disarmed them by saying, "It is not true, by the way, that I actually heard George Washington say those words in person." That's a great example of how President Reagan got followers and critics alike on his side to begin with. You win a passport to people's hearts when you PLAY YOURSELF DOWN.

Speaking of George Washington, let me be your password to one of the most astounding, little-known, best-kept secrets in the annals of American history.

On a cold, late-winter night in March of 1783 at a secret meeting place in the Hudson Valley of New York State near West Point, hundreds of officers, who were in command of the entire American Revolutionary War army, gathered for their final meeting before springing into action with a secret plot to overthrow the American government! This is a true story, as are all the stories in this book.

The roots of the plot go back to British General Cornwallis' surrender to the American commander-in-chief, General George Washington, at Yorktown in Virginia on October 17, 1781. Here's what happened after that.

General Sir Guy Carlton, commander of the other half of the British forces in America up in New York City, gave notice that he would honor Cornwallis' total surrender of the British. Unfortunately, their boss, King George III, had other ideas. He purposely stalled on signing a peace treaty.

To him, giving up his American colonies was like trying to swallow a large lump of glue. It doesn't want to go down, and leaves a very nasty taste in the mouth. Although there were no longer any military battles, General Carlton received specific orders from King George to remain in New York City until further notice. The King was apparently hoping for and expecting chaos, mob rule, and civil strife to break out in America. If it did, the British forces in New York City would be Johnny-on-the-spot and step right in to take over again when everything fell apart.

General Washington was not about to let that happen. He marched his army back up to the West Point area in New York State after Yorktown. As far as he was concerned, it would be business as usual until King George signed a peace treaty. Independence had come at too high a cost in human terms to take any chances. It had extracted a million cries of pain, built a mountain of suffering, and taken a toll of lives numbering in the twenty-five thousands.

As the months passed by, Washington's officer corps and troops grew more and more angry, however. Congress owed them months, even years, of back pay and bonuses, but was not paying up, even after an impassioned plea on behalf of his men by Washington himself. While the army was suffering loss of life and limb, and going unfed, unclothed, and unsheltered, the war was making many back in the safety and comfort of their homes fatter and richer; and arrogant enough to persist with their intellectual arguments against the war with England long after the fighting and dying began. And now Congress wanted those who had risked their lives doing the bleeding and fighting to go back to uncertain civilian lives with empty pockets -- destitute?

A group of officers, spearheaded by a Colonel Nicole, drafted a seven-page document condemning Congress as useless, and asked General Washington to be at the head of a new country as King George I of America. Washington essentially told them not to even think of such a thing.

Leaders of the officer corps began to think that a divide had opened up between the officer corps and troops on the one side, Congress and General Washington on the other side. Many felt Washington was no longer on their side.

During the next several months there were plots, intrigues, and secret meetings of the officer corps. This "Newburgh Conspiracy" of the officer corps to overthrow the government and take over America became a complex cloak and dagger affair.

Finally, the time for action arrived. The officers gathered at their secret meeting place in Newburgh next to West Point to put the final touches on their coup d'état before the bloodshed began. Most of the officer corps was there. The hall was humming with chatter and excitement. Then, suddenly and unexpectedly, the door loudly flew open. Everyone turned around. Standing right there in the doorway was the imposing, 6'- 4" tall General Washington. The hum of chatter and excitement abruptly ceased. You could hear a pin drop and feel the tension in the room, for they had now been caught red-handed by their commander-in-chief. They fully expected Washington to summon his close loyal troops to attempt to put everyone under arrest. That would be it. The bloodshed would have to begin right then and there.

That did not happen. To Washington, these men were his long-suffering stable mates. So he began in a friendly way, wearing that sincere, fatherly, close-mouthed SMILE as he walked through and greeted those near him by name, asking about their families, or wives, or kids. Other than that, he had not uttered a work. Yet, they could see that his smile was saying, "Don't worry, you are still my friends."

With their permission, he began to speak. He didn't try to wax wroth, or threaten, or bring up the tyranny and disloyalty; quite the opposite. What do you think he did? He proceeded to GIVE PRAISE AND COMPLEMENTS by telling them he was proud of their discipline and leadership during these testing and boring months waiting for a peace treaty to be signed. He told them he did not expect things to be going so well, being that they and their men had gone unpaid and were serving well beyond their enlistments, and that he certainly could not fault them for being so disgruntled.

As he began to read from a passage, he had difficulty. He stumbled over the words. The officers looked at each other with troubled expressions on their faces. Their beloved leader not only looked old and tired with his hair now turned all gray, he even sounded old and tired. Seeing their expressions, Washington humbly apologized to them. He played himself down by telling them that the war had not only made him gray-haired, but also practically blind. As he paused and fumbled with slipping spectacles over his eyes, the whole place went dead silent.

When Washington finally resumed, he said words to the effect of:

"Have we not sacrificed years of our lives and put aside our personal fears to face the noble call?" His officers nodded their heads, "YES."

"Has not our bravery and suffering now finally won us fame and glory and freedom and the respect of all the world?" His men's nods said, "YES," again.

"Do you remember the cold, the hunger, the disease, the suffering, and the death we had to bear during those terrible winters at Valley Forge and here at West Point?" The men all nodded their heads, "YES."

"Did we not do all of this so our families and children could live under freedom and liberty, not under a king or a dictator?" "YES."

From that point on, his officers did not need to hear anything else. They appeared both stunned to see their indominitable leader struggling like that, and ashamed of what they had planned to do. Washington had said nothing to which they could not say, YES.

There wasn't a dry eye in the hall. Many men had tears running down their cheeks. A few men openly wept out loud. George Washington's gray hair and failed eyes were to them a symbol of the war and its pain, its wounds, its bloodshed, its suffering, its long years away from home and children and family, its recurring nightmares about death, and .... its friends who would never return.

Like warm sun softens cold, solid ice, Washington's address softened the cold, solid determination of the conspirators. Their "coup d'état" melted away. Then it evaporated. And the breeze of emotions in that hall gently whisked it away.

The Newburgh Conspiracy was an affair that was intentionally kept quiet, but could have altered history. Few people know how close America came to being a military dictatorship, not the democratic republic we enjoy today. And, when Washington reported how close America came to having a military dictatorship, the Continental Congress panicked. They fell all over themselves to finally give the officers and the troops the money that had long been owed to them.

George Washington's preventing that coup d'état in America is one of the most superb examples in the annals of Western civilization of a great leader of character in action. And just look at it. What a wonderful example it is of our KEY # I : BEGIN BY GETTING PEOPLE ON YOUR SIDE. For the first thing Washington did was to PREPARE. He arrived at the hall in Newburgh with some prepared notes and a prop to support one of his points -- his never-before seen spectacles. Then, the second thing he did was sincerely SMILE. The third thing he did was GIVE PRAISE AND COMPLIMENTS to his officers for their discipline during the past months of uncertainty about a peace treaty. As he continued, he evoked our fourth idea, PLAY YOURSELF DOWN, by humbly confessing that the War had taken its toll on him, including practically making him blind. Fifth and finally, he drew on a technique of Socrates called the Socratic Method, that one of his favorite Romans, Cato, successfully once utilized in order to put down a similar mutiny of his army. The crux of the Socratic Method is:

5.) – GET YES ANSWERS

Like Cato, Washington began by talking about things on which he and his men agreed, like their shared pain and suffering and sacrifice, and their goal of freedom for their loved ones back home. He did not say anything to which they could not respond with a YES answer.

So, GET YES ANSWERS is the fifth way you can BEGIN BY GETTING PEOPLE ON YOUR SIDE. For, when you talk about things that compel people to answer or think YES to question after question, before they can decide whether to agree with you or cooperate with you -- they already have!

Remember this: Whatever appeals to people's eyes and ears, will readily gain admission to their minds, and get their minds on your side. When you begin by getting the mind on your side, you BEGIN BY GETTING PEOPLE ON YOUR SIDE, and you get the thinking of people moving in a positive psychological direction. All their nerves and muscles and bodily organs are wide open to receive what you want to tell them. Whereas, on the other hand, if they are not on your side to begin with -- if they are thinking NO deep down inside -- their neuromuscular systems withdraw into a state of rejection. They automatically are psychologically against what you tell them. And, like a large ship at sea, a person's large personal pride, once moving in a certain direction, does not easily turn or change course. It would require the patience and powers of Providence to change those people and make them want to cooperate with you willingly so that they will not just follow your orders and go through the motions, but do the best they can do and be the best they can be.

So start today. Think of what you have to do and PREPARE in your mind what to say to people. Greet everyone with a SMILE, not a business-as-usual facial expression. Look people straight in the eyes. You'll find something to GIVE PRAISE AND COMPLIMENTS about, sincerely. Remember, everyone is in some way your superior. So praise them and PLAY YOURSELF DOWN. Be humble. They will love you for it. And don't forget to use the Socratic Method -- GET YES ANSWERS -- if the situation arises. If you start to do these things today, I promise you will be like a magnet. Your followers will be attracted to you.

To be a great real-life leader of character, implement:

KEY # 1 : BEGIN BY GETTING PEOPLE ON YOUR SIDE.

In this chapter I showed you five simple ways to do that:

1.) - PREPARE.

2.) - SMILE.

3.) - GIVE PRAISE AND COMPLIMENTS.

4.) - PLAY YOURSELF DOWN.

5.) - GET YES ANSWERS.

35

Chapter 3: Do This ... And It Will Work Wonders For You

On a chilly, overcast day in March of 1981, America was hit with a shocking bombshell. President Ronald Reagan, in office just nine weeks, lay close to sudden and violent death at George Washington University Hospital in Washington DC, with a bullet from the gun of an assassin lodged one inch from his heart. During his recovery after the operation to remove the bullet, the President's life still being a close call, his White House staff came into the hospital, en-mass, to visit him. This was a kind gesture by people who loved, respected, and followed him. But, it was a mistake, like leaving the front door of the store open with no one home. Reagan's reaction, even in his mentally and physically shaky condition, showed why people love, respect, and followed him. When he looked around and saw that all of his key White House staff had made the mistake of being there at the same time, did he condemn them or criticize them or read them the riot act over their foolish mistake? No, he did no such thing. He <u>corrected</u> them by simply saying, "Who's minding the store?" With that, there was dead silence. Everyone clammed up. Half of the people left. They all immediately got the point. And, here is my point. To get people to voluntarily <u>want</u> to follow you or cooperate with you <u>willingly,</u> be sure you do what Ronald Reagan did that day, and on many other occasions, which is, follow our:

<u>KEY # 2 : CORRECT PEOPLE WITHOUT CONDEMNING OR CRITICIZING</u>

Throughout his political life, from 1964 to 1989, this was one of the hallmarks of human relations and leadership that Ronald

Reagan consistently followed. It's one that I want you to follow. But, how do you know exactly how to correct without condemning or criticizing? I will now show you four ways to do that.

On that day in the hospital when Ronald Reagan looked around and saw that all of his White House staff were there at the same time, he used what turns out to be the first of our four ways to CORRECT PEOPLE WITHOUT CONDEMNING OR CRITICIZING, which is:

1.) - CALL ATTENTION TO PEOPLE'S MISTAKES INDIRECTLY.

Ronald Reagan poignantly called attention to his staff's mistake indirectly with the simple words, "Who's minding the store?" When they made their second mistake -- trying to justify their actions -- telling him, don't worry, the government is running just as it would be if you were there, he responded with, "What makes you think that would make me feel better?" He injected a bit of double entendre humor into the situation in order to CALL ATTENTION TO PEOPLES MISTAKES INDIRECTLY a second time.

That was vintage Ronald Reagan. He was a wonderworker at getting people to _want_ to follow him and cooperate with him _willingly_ because, for one thing, he always looked for a way to get around condemning and criticizing people when they made mistakes. He won a passport to their hearts by always trying to CALL ATTENTION TO PEOPLE'S MISTAKES INDIRECTLY rather than rub their noses into their mistakes.

Back in the 1700's, Thomas Jefferson also always prudently avoided rubbing people's noses into their mistakes, always making certain to CALL ATTENTION TO PEOPLE'S MISTAKES INDIRECTLY. Here's an example of how he did that.

This was the summer of 1784. Thomas Jefferson joined with Benjamin Franklin and John Adams in Europe for two years to negotiate agreements for the newly independent American states. He remained in France himself as Foreign Minister, observing life over there as if it were a precursor to how America might someday be. He made a conscious effort to calculate how the things he observed would affect America, Virginia, and his family. There was much he observed and liked. There was also much he disliked: squalor and corruption in cities; great masses of poverty-stricken people; workers being exploited in factories; miserable living conditions; moral depravity; adulterous intrigues that made marital love less than sacrosanct; lust for sex and luxury that was destructive to health.

Despite France's moral ills, Jefferson readily soaked up its culture. He was finally coming out of the prolonged depression that gripped him after the death of his sweet, trim, graceful, personable wife and true love and best friend, Martha, back in September 1782 at the youthful age of 33 years. But he still missed her. He also deeply missed his two young children, Martha and Maria. The changing mores that he saw in France's "garden of life" also made him deeply worried about his two young girls.

His sister-in-law back in Virginia was keeping him up to date on Martha's and Maria's own changing mores, you know, the problems and mistakes that come with growing up. He knew his nurturing hand was needed to make sure the two flowers in his own little "garden of life" back in Virginia were growing straight and smelling sweet, but he could not be there in person to prune them and nurture them. So, he began having fatherly talks with them by mail to prune them and nurture them. Did he condemn or criticize them? Absolutely not. Here is some of the inspirational pruning and nurturing he did in letters to his two blossoming "flowers":

"Youth is a time when great exertions are necessary, but you have little time left to make them."
"Idleness begets boredom, boredom begets depression, and depression begets a diseased body."

"If at any moment you catch yourself in idleness, start from it -- draw back from it -- as if from the edge of a cliff."

"My expectations from you are high. Resolve and hard work are all you need to attain them."

"Of all the cancers of human happiness, none corrodes with so silent yet so destructive a tooth as laziness."

"The Almighty has never made known when he created life and when he will put an end to it. You can only prepare for that event by never saying or doing a bad thing. Follow your conscience, that faithful internal monitor which our Maker has given all of us."

How masterful! Jefferson knew it was wise to CALL ATTENTION TO PEOPLE'S MISTAKES INDIRECTLY in order to constructively CORRECT PEOPLE WITHOUT CONDEMNING OR CRITICIZING.

Here is another piece of human relations wisdom and great real-life leadership of character that the intellectual father of our country always tried to implement. It's the second way that you can CORRECT PEOPLE WITHOUT CONDEMNING OR CRITICIZING.

2.) – MAKE PEOPLE'S MISTAKES SEEM EASY TO CORRECT.

Earlier in Thomas and Martha Jefferson's married life, Thomas' best friend, Dabney Carr, who was married to Thomas' sister, also named Martha, suddenly and unexpectedly died from a massive attack of typhoid fever at just twenty-nine years of age. From that day forward, Thomas Jefferson and wife Martha kept his distraught sister and her six children with them in their house, Monticello. They took it upon themselves to raise and educate the children as their own.

A few years later, Thomas Jefferson became their legal guardian, and he began to pay special attention to the education of his nephew, Peter Carr. So, it's no wonder that he almost felt like a man told he has a terminal illness when, during the time he was over in Europe as Foreign Minister, he learned from home that Peter knew more about the subtle snares of the devil like playing high-card and horse-shoes than he knew about Homer and hyperbolas. Peter could not avoid falling hopelessly behind in his studies.

Thus, Jefferson began to dispatch fatherly letters to him. Did he scold or condemn Peter in those letters for his mistake? No. Thomas Jefferson would always find a way to MAKE PEOPLE'S MISTAKES SEEM EASY TO CORRECT. Here's how he did so when it came to Peter Carr. He succinctly told young Peter that "the fortunes of our lives depend on employing well the short period of youth," and therefore, "time now begins to be precious to you"; and, he outlined an ingenious course of study and reading that would enable Peter to catch up.

It worked like a charm. With this guidance, Peter was able to correct his mistake, get back on track, and go on to follow in his uncle's footsteps. He successfully accomplished the same sequence of studies at the College of William and Mary, and studied under some of the same tutors, that Thomas Jefferson did.

Now. Let's revisit the Socratic Method that we talked about under KEY #1 in the last chapter. When people who have never studied or even heard of Socrates inadvertently MAKE PEOPLE'S MISTAKES SEEM EASY TO CORRECT by simply asking questions instead of condemning or criticizing, little do they know they are actually employing the Socratic Method, that great ancient philosopher's favorite leadership method. I can vividly remember being corrected that way by my Mom and Dad at home when I was growing up in Paterson, New Jersey, instead of being criticized or chewed out. Here are a couple of simple everyday situations that occurred in my own life, and probably in yours, that will illustrate my point.

Do the following scenarios ring a bell with you? You come home from playing ball or just hanging out, anything but cutting the grass as you were told to do -- the day before. Your Mom or your Dad inadvertently uses the Socratic method by simply saying something like this to you, "I know you must have forgotten that you were supposed to cut the grass yesterday, right?" Like, say no more. Knowing what's good for you, you wisely proceed to correct yesterday's mistake. You immediately hustle out to the garage for the lawn mower and start to cut the grass. You have just been let off the hook because your Mom or your Dad wanted to MAKE PEOPLE'S MISTAKES SEEM EASY TO CORRECT.

Or, perhaps you are watching reruns of "MASH" or "Happy Days" or your currently favorite TV program, or playing a game on the computer on the evening of a school day. You have not yet started on your homework. As time rolls by, your Mom or your Dad reminds you of your mistake, not by condemning or criticizing or hollering at you. Mom or Dad know right well that you know that they know there is no way they can actually help you with your math homework, but they proceed to just ask you this simple but effective question anyway, "Do you need some help with your homework?" You get the point. You can't put it off any longer. You pack it in with what you're doing and switch gears to thinking about today's math assignment. And, you realize that you have just been let off the hook.

Your Mom, or your Dad, has just used MAKE PEOPLE'S MISTAKES SEEM EASY TO CORRECT, our second way to CORRECT PEOPLE WITHOUT CONDEMNING OR CRITICIZING. They have instinctively used the Socratic Method of asking a question rather than scolding or flying off the handle.

Being let off the hook brings to mind the famous West Point graduate, Mexican War hero, Civil War general, and college president -- Robert E. Lee. He has been a constant source of inspiration to me ever since, starting in 1973, I had read biographies of him by Douglas Southall Freeman and others.

Do you know what the secret of Robert E. Lee's amazing popularity was, and why he has continued to command respect, inspiration, and staying power in the eyes of history, despite having been on the losing side of the American Civil War? The secret was simply his trying to be a great real-life leader of character. It was his knowing how to handle men.

Here's one story, from many that I have read in Robert E. Lee's biographies that will give you an idea of what I mean.

This takes place at our United States military Academy -- West Point -- several years before our American Civil War. At that time, Robert E. Lee was still a colonel in the US Army. He was the superintendent (college president) of West Point.

Folks who happened to linger at the parade ground one day after a cadet review were aghast at what they witnessed. Amidst a cloud of dust, and grass flying up all over the place, and a crowd of cadets cheering and shouting, there were two cadets rolling around the ground, punching and bloodying each other!

Cadet Archibald Gracie from New York was getting the worst of it from the southern Cadet Wharton Green. Therefore, it was Gracie who ended up getting caught, as Green and the rest of the cadets scattered to escape an instructor who was rushing over to halt the embarrassing ruckus. When Gracie was asked the name of the cadet with whom he was fighting, his answer was, "You will have to ask him, for I'm no informer." He was immediately put on report and in detention, which was kind of like being arrested.

The very next morning there was a knock on Superintendent Lee's door. It was Wharton Green, the cadet who got away. When Lee gave him permission to enter and permission to speak, Green said, "Mr. Gracie was yesterday reported for fighting ... the other fellow was not."

To that, Lee surmised, "And I presume you are the other fellow?"

Green confirmed that he was the other fellow, and asked, "Don't you think it very hard on him, Colonel, to have to bear all of the penalty incidents, being he also got the worst of the fracas? I wish to submit that for your consideration."

Lee confirmed to cadet Green that he would allow what he just said to be entered as a deposition, and asked him what he would suggest. Green answered, "Simply this, Sir. Whatever punishment is meted out to him, I insist on having the same given to me."

Lee was duly impressed. "The offense entails a heavy penalty," he warned.

To that, Green replied, "I am aware of the fact, Sir, but Mr. Gracie is not entitled to a monopoly of it."

Lee agreed. Then, like an angry but caring father, he took the opportunity to MAKE PEOPLE'S MISTAKES SEEM EASY TO CORRECT by asking Green if he would also agree, for the future, "that it is better for brothers to dwell together in peace and harmony."

Green replied with a simple, "Yes, Colonel."

This is the point at which Superintendent Lee let them both off the hook. Because Cadet Green agreed -- and because he already knew that Cadet Gracie, who stood to get the worst of the punishment for having started the fight, had already also agreed -- Lee said that he would, in that case, completely remove the report from <u>both</u> cadets' records. He would punish <u>neither</u> cadet.

With that, Cadet Green voluntarily proffered a statement that showed Robert E. Lee was already sowing the seeds of respect and great leadership of character, right there on that small but famous post called West Point, that would someday grow into the respect from, and great leadership of, whole armies of men on other days in other places having other now famous names. The statement that Cadet Green proffered that morning after agreeing that it is far better for brothers to dwell in peace was: "And if we were all like you, Sir, it would be an easy thing to do."

When you MAKE PEOPLE'S MISTAKES SEEM EASY TO CORRECT in order to <u>CORRECT PEOPLE WITHOUT CONDEMNING OR CRITICIZING</u>, like President Reagan or your Mom and Dad or Robert E. Lee did, you give people -- kind of like a judge gives a light sentence to people who are first time offenders -- the opportunity to do what is necessary to correct their mistakes themselves. That gives them new life, which allows them to learn from their mistakes.

Great leaders of character spare other people's pride by letting them save face. That tends to make other people gratefully <u>want</u> to <u>willingly</u> cooperate with them and follow them, rather than want to rebel and "give them a piece of their mind" as they would if their pride were injured and their intelligence were offended. I remember learning that lesson one day from my high school football coach, Nelson Graham, when I was his first string quarterback on the Central High School football team in Paterson, New Jersey.

That year was the first winning season Central High School had in ten years! We were on a five-game winning streak one Saturday afternoon on our home field at Paterson's famous Hinchliffe Stadium. It was first and ten for us on Lyndhurst's four-yard line with only a minute left in the game. We were losing by a score of 12 – 7, and had no timeouts left. Our coach, Nelson Graham, was a college All-American halfback at Muhlenberg College and a jet pilot with the rank of major in the Air Force Reserve. He came down on the side of the players over what, in those years, was an ongoing dispute in high school football circles about changes in the rules pertaining to whether the game should, or should not, be kept totally in the hands of the players on the field. So, as his quarterback -- his "field general" -- I called all the plays myself on the field in the huddle during games.

Coach Graham always told me that, in such a situation, I should give the ball to our big 6'- 4", 250- pound fullback, Pat Dilemma, who later went on to play at Rutgers. So, in the huddle, I called his number.

Lyndhurst was good. They had been "submarining" and "shooting the gaps" all day long against Dilemma, taking his legs out, and holding him to gains of a yard or two -- or a loss. We ran the play, and they did it again. It was now second down on the three yard line. Time was running out. I called

Dilemma's number again, and broke the huddle. This would be the last play of the game. When I yelled, "all set," and our line went down into their three-point stance, I saw Lyndhurst's defensive ends move to a position to shoot-in on an inside slant - - inside of our ends who now were not allowed to move a muscle. They again had five down-lineman and four linebackers right in the gaps between their linemen, all bunched up inside the ends to stuff our big fullback. So, I decided to call our "audible", which went like this: If I called out, "jets," it changed the play into a quick pitchout to the halfback who would sprint full-speed around the end. If I called out, "horses," it changed the play to a handoff into the middle of the line. I turned right and called out, "jets." I turned left and yelled, "jets." At the snap of the ball from the center, I immediately lateralled the usual fast, underhand, spiral, line drive pitchout to our speedy left halfback, Olin Brown. It was a perfect pitchout, but it bounced off of his hip. He never turned his head and hands toward me to catch the ball. He had not heard me yell "jets" to change the play.

Lyndhurst's defensive end was right there to pounce on the fumble. It was their ball, first and ten. The clock ran out. The game was over. We lost.

In the locker room after the game, half the team told me I made the right call; the other half gave me the cold shoulder and blamed me for our loss. What a downer! I had a hard time sleeping all that weekend. I had a hard time concentrating to do my homework.

During the following Monday's practice, the coach did something unusual. Instead of the usual light workout, we had a full game-like scrimmage. At one point, after having his head together with the defensive coach at the five yard line, Coach Graham came over to our huddle and told me to run the fast-pitchout play I had audiblized-to with "jets" at the end of Saturday's game. The coaches had watched the game films. I saw they had set up the defense exactly like Lyndhurst's was set up in the game. This time, Olin Brown caught my pitchout. He started sprinting full-speed toward the corner of the end zone from the five yard line. Then he finished up actually just jogging slowly into the end zone. It was a cakewalk. No one got even close to him.

Coach Graham said to the whole team, "That's how it would have worked in the game if the crowd noise had not prevented Brown from hearing Remick yell, 'jets'." He complimented me by saying: "That was a smart call, Remick. Brown could have done that in the game. We would have won!"

You don't know how good I felt. Coach Graham eliminated the division between his players, and let me save face. Without criticizing or condemning, he corrected the whole team for being divided, he corrected Olin Brown for not looking at me during the game, and he corrected me for taking the chance to audible over the crowd noise.

The team came together again. We went on to win our traditional big Thanksgiving Day game against our cross-city rival, Eastside High School, for the first time in ten years in front of an overflow stadium of about 15,000 people.

I have never forgotten that incident. Sometimes I relive it as a nightmare; I never forgot how important it can be to:

3.) - LET PEOPLE SAVE FACE.

And that's the third thing you should do when you : <u>CORRECT PEOPLE WITHOUT CONDEMNING OR CRITICIZING</u>.

Do you know what was one of the bitterest days in the history of our country? It was that tragic day in April of 1865 when, shortly after 10 p.m., President Abraham Lincoln took a fatal bullet to the head, shot from the pistol of a well-known actor, John Wilkes Booth, while watching a performance of the popular comedy, "Our American Cousin", at Ford's Theatre in Washington, DC. Lincoln died in the rooming house directly across the street from the theater at 7:22 a.m. the next day, without ever regaining consciousness. According to *The Complete Works of Abraham Lincoln* by Nicolay and Hay, and several other books on Lincoln, Secretary of War Edwin Stanton proclaimed at Lincoln's bedside, "There lays the most perfect ruler of man that the world has ever seen." But, was Lincoln always perfect? Oh no, in fact, here is a superb example for you of what <u>not</u> to do -- of how to turn perfect strangers into mortal enemies -- courtesy of Abraham Lincoln, himself.

The story takes place in Springfield, Illinois when Abraham Lincoln was a young practicing lawyer. He thought that he could make a political name for himself by criticizing and attacking politicians in letters that he would get published in newspapers. Then one day, he learned a lesson he would never forget.

It was in 1842 that Lincoln made the mistake of condemning, criticizing, and humiliating a scrappy politician named James Shields in a letter published in the *Springfield Journal* newspaper. Shields was incensed. Somehow, he found out that the letter was from this young upstart lawyer named Abraham Lincoln. What did Shields do? He challenged Lincoln to a duel! And he boldly gave Lincoln the choice of weapons.

Lincoln was duly shocked. He was also stuck. He could not very well publicly "chicken out" because he was trying to make a name for himself. So, under duress, he accepted the challenge. He chose swords as the weapon because he knew a West Point graduate who offered to give him lessons.

After minimal practice, the fatal day arrived. Lincoln and Shields faced off and were ready to carve each other up in a fight to the death on a sand bar in the Mississippi River. With the infamous pistol duel between Alexander Hamilton and Aaron Burr that resulted in Hamilton's death probably passing through everyone's mind, the "seconds" for Lincoln and Shields interrupted to put a stop to the madness. They emphasized that it was their choice, not Lincoln's or Shields' choice. Therefore, each man's honor would be preserved. Under those conditions, both Lincoln and Shields agreed to halt the duel. Both men not only avoided butchering each other, but ultimately, each let the other man save face. Abraham Lincoln never forgot that nightmarish, near life-ending experience. He had to learn the hard way. And he never forgot it is important to LET PEOPLE SAVE FACE, as you will also see later in the chapter.

Years later, in 1861, now <u>President</u> Abraham Lincoln and now <u>General</u> Robert E. Lee became embroiled in the American Civil War, on opposite sides. It didn't have to be that way. Lincoln had offered Lee the Field Command of the Union Army, but Lee turned him down. Here's why.

Lee was against any civil war, to start with. Like Lincoln, he opposed secession. Therefore, he was opposed to his native Virginia seceding from the Union, even though he believed that they had the sovereign right to do so. And he also thought that it was wrong for the Union army to invade his native Virginia or any other state that seceded. He said, if it did, he would be forced to resign his Commission. And, if it did, he would not fight against his family and friends in Virginia, and would, on the contrary, be forced to defend his home and State. As we know, it did -- and he did.

The history of General Robert E. Lee's campaigns after he personally took over field command of the Confederate Army is the story of a military and leadership genius who set all of his talent at strategy and tactics, and his magnificent leadership and generalship, against Federal Union Armies that were always far superior in numbers, supplies, and equipment. For eighteen months after he took over field command, he and his right arm, Stonewall Jackson, prevailed in battle after battle. First came their shattering repulse of the huge Union Army that was lodged outside of the Confederate capital in Richmond, Virginia during the Seven Days Campaign in June 1862. They went from there to battles bearing the names Second Manassas, Bull Run, Antietam, Fredricksburg, and Chancellorsville to kick butt.

Then came the fateful confrontation near a small town in Pennsylvania called Gettysburg that was innocently sparked-off when a Confederate Army detachment peacefully went into town looking to buy direly needed shoes. It was during Lee's thrust into the North, an invasion that was meant to spook the Lincoln administration into a peace treaty that would stop the war and simply allow the new Confederate States of America to live in peace and self-determination.

Lee's strategy at Gettysburg was the same clever, unconventional, audaciously aggressive strategy that he had successfully used to "kick butt" in all of those previous battles. He always implemented surprise, creativity, and lightning fast reaction time to neutralize the huge superiority in numbers the Union armies enjoyed, beating them to the punch at securing the available tactical battlefield advantages. Lee and Stonewall Jackson both aggressively thought "out of the box". And when Lee gave the order to move, he could eminently count on Jackson to instinctively react immediately to execute the most daring of operations with aggressive shock and awe. Jackson understood that speed and timing meant everything. But now Jackson was gone -- killed at Chancellorsville in foggy woodlands by accidental friendly fire. And Lee had no other Stonewall Jacksons. His great mistake was thinking he did.

Lee thought his other generals could fill Jackson's shoes. They were good in many ways. But when he needed them at Gettysburg to step up, as Jackson would have done, they were not there. They were not daring like Jackson was. They were cautious and procrastinating. Some historians have even contended that their procrastination bordered on insubordination. Their minds simply were not on the same wavelength as Lee's. Lee and Jackson were like hammers. The others were like anvils. They did not work from the same audaciously aggressive playbook as Lee and Jackson. Both Lee and Jackson played offense. Lee's other commanders liked to play containment defense.

Despite Lee's riding up and down the lines at Gettysburg, flat out prodding his generals, saying, "I think you had better move (now)," and reminding them that the entire plan depended, as in past victories, on speed, surprise, and timing, his generals were surly and sluggish. They were slow to move. By the time they did, "the train had left the station." It was too late to execute Lee's plan. They had blown the tactical advantages of time, place, and circumstance that were Lee's trademarks. Their golden opportunity had passed. They gave the disorganized Union forces time to get reorganized, occupy the high ground, and become reinforced with massive amounts of men, munitions, and artillery pieces. We know all of this now, in hindsight. Lee, and the brigades commanded by General Pickett that were saddled with the task of breaching the center of the Union lines, had to find out under an onslaught of fire -- and too late -- what's known as the hard way.

The charge of Pickett's three brigades is reminiscent of the ill-fated British "Charge of the Light Brigade" that was made forever famous in literature by Alfred Lord Tennyson. However, "Pickett's Charge" was probably the most important, daring, gallant, picturesque, and magnificent charge ever made in warfare.

Pickett's devoted troops began the one mile charge toward the Union line like soldiers on parade. They marched through cornfields and across meadows with banners proudly flying and fixed bayonets glittering and reflecting the sunlight. The Union troops viewed the grandeur that was approaching them and their literal "shooting gallery" with amazement.

Maintaining parade-like order, Pickett's troops continued to sweep forward, then broke into an easy trot, ignoring the holes now being blown in their lines by devastating Union cannon-fire. Then, with Pickett's swashbuckling brigade commander General Armistead in the lead waving his black hat on the tip of his sword, the troops broke into a run, letting out with their fearful rebel yell. As they did, they were blasted face-to-face by Union canister. And, the Union infantry opened up on them with barrage after barrage of deadly musket-fire from behind the stone wall on Cemetery Ridge -- point blank.

Now, huge numbers of men were being bowled over by the waves of musket-fire. It looked like they were being swallowed up by quicksand. But, there was no quicksand. They were simply laid-out on the ground, flat and dead. If it were not for the shrieks and screams of the wounded and dying, you would not know they were there. They were disappearing. E.P.

Alexander, on Union-held Seminary Ridge, observed in horror, "Human life was being poured out like water."

At one point during the battle, Armistead, still waving hat on sword in a confident, swashbuckling way, and some of his brigade, actually <u>did</u> breach the Union line. Vaulting the stone wall, they planted their battle flags and declared victory. But it was short-lived. The Union side was not about to give up. Why? I'll tell you why. It's because the surly sluggardness and procrastination that had previously allowed time for massive Union reinforcements came back to bite the Confederates. Two more Union regiments were quickly rushed in. They closed the breach and surrounded the Confederates who had planted the battle flag. It was a massacre worse than Custer's Last Stand.

General Armistead went down, mortally wounded. Thousands went down with him, or were captured. And, what I am going to tell you next is astounding. Every single soldier in the University Grays -- all college students from "Ole Miss" -- was killed in the face of that onslaught by the unexpected Union reinforcements!

When the dust settled after the fighting at Gettysburg on those first three days in July of 1863, the Union Army had lost 23,000 of its 95,000 men. It was even worse for Lee's Confederate Army. They lost 28,000 of only 75,000 men. Four out of five soldiers in Pickett's magnificent division were killed in a matter of minutes during the single charge. The grandest-ever charge was a day late and a dollar short. That bloodiest-ever charge turned out to be nothing more than a forlorn hope. Confederate pride and daring shook hands with disaster that day.

Lee rode out to meet the shattered fragments of his Army. Broken-up men hobbled and stumbled away from the debacle, dispirited and disillusioned. It was ugly. But, do you know what was not ugly, but was one of the most magnificent and magnanimous things that history has recorded about Robert E. Lee's great real-life leadership of character? Despite the fact that, in the end, only eleven of Lee's brigades carried the fight, while the rest of his twenty-seven brigades sat it out and never joined the battle, and despite the failure of his generals to respond to his orders, he did not condemn them, or criticize them, or chastise them, or humiliate them in the heat of the moment in front of their troops. He allowed his great real-life leadership of character and what he always considered to be a categorically imperative human relations principle, LET PEOPLE SAVE FACE, first work its magic. For he knew that he could <u>CORRECT PEOPLE WITHOUT CONDEMNING OR CRITICIZING</u> at another time, in another place.

As the small groups of bloodied and beaten troops found their way back to the Confederate side, here's what else few leaders in all of history have had the character to do. Granted, his generals had made the mistake of being almost insubordinate in their procrastination and surly sluggardness at executing their commander-in-chief's battle orders. In hindsight, though, he realized that <u>he</u> had also made the mistake of not recognizing that they were not Stonewall Jackson. And at that point in time , he was also thinking about how to defend against a possible counter-attack, and further down the road of war, how to bounce back to achieve future victories after the Gettysburg disaster. So, besides letting his generals save face with the troops as they drifted by, you won't believe what else he did. He actually put the blame on himself! He shouted out these words to his troops in earshot of his generals:

"You have done all that you could do .... the fault is entirely my own .... all this is my fault .... it is I who have lost this fight .... get together and let us do the best we can toward saving which is left to us .... this has been my fight, and upon my shoulders rests all the blame."

Seeing and hearing that, the battered troops forming up into precautionary defensive positions, and even badly wounded men being carried off on stretchers took off their hats and, waving them, cheered Robert E. Lee as he rode by.

You're probably asking, "Why in Heaven's name did Robert E. Lee take the blame?" Here's why. He knew he had to and wanted to confront and correct his generals at some point. But, he believed it important to <u>CORRECT PEOPLE WITHOUT CONDEMNING OR CRITICIZING</u>. The last thing he wanted to do was crush his generals' confidence in their present tenuous frame of mind. The Battle of Gettysburg had already done too much of that. It was critical that they continue to <u>want</u> to follow him <u>willingly</u>. And, throughout his life, he had learned that it is not as difficult for people to swallow their pride and listen to their mistakes being corrected when the person doing the correcting has swallowed his own pride and humbly admitted that he has been less than perfect himself. Besides, remember what the old saw says, "The barber always lathers a man before he shaves him." Those are the leadership principles that Robert E. Lee stuck to that day when he nobly sacrificed his pride and lifelong reputation by putting the blame on himself.

I'm not telling you to unnecessarily put the blame on yourself for mistakes made or caused by others, as Lee did. You don't need to be a martyr to be a great real-life leader. But, let's face it. We all make many mistakes during our lives. A few words humbling ourselves can speak volumes to people. It can turn adversarial people into friends and followers. So, the fourth way to <u>CORRECT PEOPLE WITHOUT CONDEMNING OR CRITICIZING</u>, like Robert E. Lee was not afraid to do throughout his life, is:

4.) – FIRST TALK ABOUT MISTAKES YOU HAVE MADE.

Because of Union General Meade's great respect for Robert E. Lee's proven ability to snatch victory from the jaws of defeat, the Union Army never did counterattack that day after the Confederates limped back to their lines. In fact, that night on the Union side, General Meade was warily bracing for another possible Confederate attack, thinking that Lee would never allow his generals to do that to him again, or something like that.

That night on the Confederate side, Lee could be heard in a loud and sorrowful voice, letting out a forlorn lament that was almost reminiscent of the one Jesus let out from the Cross to God in Heaven. Lee was heard crying out progressively louder and louder: "Too bad!.....<u>TOO BAD!</u> .... <u>OH!</u> .... <u>TOO, TOO BAD!</u>"

A few days later, south of Gettysburg in Washington, D.C., President Lincoln was also saying "Too bad," but for different reasons. He was lamenting that General Meade did not immediately counterattack Lee. Whatsmore, because of the torrential rains, Meade's continued pursuit of what was left of Lee's army got bogged down. That allowed "The Gray Fox" and his entire Confederate Army to slip back across the Potomac River and escape back home into Virginia.

President Lincoln was urged by "advisors" (which undoubtedly included his nagging wife) to write a blistering letter of condemnation to Meade. He did not have to think about it very long to see the mistake his "advisors" were making in condemning Meade and urging him to do the same. No one knew all the facts out there on the ground but Meade. Such a letter would likely trigger Meade's resignation. And, let's face it. Meade was the first general to record a success against Lee in a dismal past eighteen months of the War. And, what a momentous success it was!

So Lincoln corrected that mistake of his "advisors" the same way he had been correcting people's mistakes ever since the near life-ending experience he had as a young lawyer back in Illinois fighting a sword duel over a mistake <u>he</u> had made, and never ceased to regret. Much like Lee, he stuck to the principle, FIRST TALK ABOUT MISTAKES YOU HAVE MADE. And that's what he did.

A famous, mildly written, non-condemning letter about Gettysburg to General Meade was found among Abraham Lincoln's papers after his death, as reported in *The Complete Works of Abraham Lincoln*. But, even that letter was never sent to Meade.

Almost two years later, on April 7, 1865, now Union Commanding General Ulysses S. Grant would also write a famous, non-condemning letter. This one was to Confederate General Robert E. Lee, just outside of a town called Appomattox Court House in Virginia.

For almost two years, Lee's army had been almost magically avoiding being crushed and defeated by Grant's armies that now had up to five times as many men. It was reminiscent of how General George Washington, another Virginian, had magically avoided being crushed by the hugely superior British armies during the Revolutionary War while efforts were afoot to garner help from the French.

The Confederate Army was badly bleeding and rapidly shrinking and crumbling under the shear weight of battle after battle with little to no food or supplies. Grant had slowly but inexorably whittled-down Lee's armies to less than 28,000 fighting men.

Grant was very smart. He could "read" Lee. He knew and respected Lee's immense character. Because of that he felt certain that Lee had to be thinking that he was making a serious, serious mistake continuing with the horrible and irreplaceable loss of men in what had to more and more look like a lost and hopeless cause against the Union's absolutely overwhelming might.

So, as revealed in his celebrated book, *Personal Memoirs*, Grant wrote his mild, non-condemning letter to Lee in such a way as to CALL ATTENTION TO PEOPLE'S MISTAKES INDIRECTLY using the following compelling words:

"The results of the last week must convince you of the hopelessness of further resistance. ….. I regard it as my duty to shift from myself the responsibility of the further effusion of blood."

In other words, he indirectly told Lee that he was making a monumental mistake by thinking there was any possibility that the Confederate Army could avoid being completely annihilated, down to the last man, if the fighting continued.

Then Grant went on to MAKE PEOPLE'S MISTAKES SEEM EASY TO CORRECT by offering a cessation of what was becoming little more than a Union hunt-and-kill operation, if Lee would surrender his Army.

On Palm Sunday, April 9, 1865, Lee and Grant sat down in the living room of the Wilbur McLean house in Appomattox, with the Union Army on one side of the village, and Lee's ragged little Army on the other side. One Union officer commented on how miserable and half-starved the Confederate soldiers looked, "It was a sad sight," he said, "a scene to melt the bravest heart."

Ulysses S. Grant displayed great real-life leadership of character once again when he implemented the principle, LET PEOPLE SAVE FACE, by putting out orders to do nothing to humiliate the Confederate soldiers who had fought so bravely in spite of being in desperate shape for so many months. And he let Lee save face by allowing him to retain his sword, implying between soldiers that even the best of men can sometimes be the loser.

Grant allowed Lee's officers the face-saving gesture of retaining their side arms and horses. He permitted every man who was using his own horse or mule to take the animal home to aid him with putting in the crop "to carry themselves and their families through the next winter".

For four years, they had been doing everything they could to kill Lee's men. Now Grant was doing whatever he could to keep them alive and healthy by making it possible for them to get their spring crops into the ground. And, when word of Robert E. Lee's surrender leaked out to the Union lines, provoking an in-your-face, one hundred gun victory salute, Grant quickly sent out orders to put an immediate stop to it. He said, "The Confederates were now our prisoners, and we did not want to exult over their downfall."

During their meeting, Lee embarrassingly confessed that his army was "in very sad condition for want of food". In the spirit of FIRST TALK ABOUT MISTAKES YOU HAVE MADE, Grant also confessed, "As for forage, we had ourselves depended almost entirely upon the country." But Grant had just recently beaten the Confederates in a race to a Confederate train at Appomattox Station, loaded with provisions intended to rescue Lee's army from starvation. He authorized his quartermaster to give Lee 25,000 rations.

At Appomattox (where not a shot was fired), even more than in great battlefield victories like Bull Run and Chancellorsville for Lee, and Vicksburg for Grant, West Point graduates Robert E. Lee and Ulysses S. Grant both showed the true measure of what it means to be a great real-life leader of character. Their leadership during the closing days of the Civil War probably did more than anything else to heal the deep wounds in America and bring "Jimmy Jones" of Pennsylvania and his brother "Johnny Jones" of Virginia, who fought on opposite sides in the war, back together again.

Not the battles Lee and Grant had been schooled at West Point and in the Army to fight, but the values and character they had inculcated at West Point, and the great practical real-life techniques of leadership that they went on to learn, have been proven by history to be the hidden jewels in the crown of each man's career. One of those practical techniques of leadership was: <u>CORRECT PEOPLE WITHOUT CONDEMNING OR CRITICIZING</u>.

Like Lee and Grant, Abraham Lincoln also knew how deadly it is to condemn, criticize, nag, or belittle someone. Oh, did he ever know that! His assassination was one of America's greatest tragedies. But most people don't know that before his assassination, he had already been dying the death of a thousand cuts. For, although he was ecstatically happy when he was first married, Mary Todd Lincoln soon fell into criticizing, nagging, faulting, and nit-picking the life and love out of him for the next 23 years. Only death brought him lasting peace.

Lincoln and his wife were as different as chalk and cheese. He was quiet, reserved, and low key. She was hyperactive and foolishly jealous. Early in their marriage, she began to nag him and humiliate him in front of other people. He slowly but surely began to jump ship whenever he could. For example, during his early lawyering years in Springfield, Illinois, the other attorneys who were out on the circuit, as he was, would make sure they got back home to spend the weekends with their wives. Not Lincoln, however. He would intentionally take "shore leave" from his ship of marriage by arranging to see additional clients on weekends.

When he became President, first lady Mary Todd Lincoln would criticize him and find fault with him because of the Union army defeats at the hands of General Robert E. Lee during the Civil War. Her criticizing and condemning and badgering President Lincoln over his selection of commanding generals helped create what became somewhat of a revolving door of field commanders early in the War. That tended to keep the morale of the "Private Jimmy Joneses" from Pennsylvania on a roller coaster ride while firing up the morale of the "Private Johnny Joneses" from Virginia.

Mrs. Lincoln's criticizing and finding fault slowly changed her husband's feelings for her and made him regret ever having signed on to their ship of marriage that had become a ship of horrors to him. It was so sad that, compared to his loving thoughts of the long ago, he now sometimes could barely stand the sight of her. The criticizing and condemning created a sad relationship that eventually rubbed out all of their cherished moments like an eraser. In the end, it was said about Lincoln, "Twas not just losing love that tortured his days, but that it was lost in such little ways."

Personally, I can look back on my own life and see (because I was preoccupied with getting my English employees to cooperate willingly) how I myself had not yet come to completely understand how utterly useless and foolish, and even dangerous, it can be to condemn or criticize people, even if they deserve it.

It is useless and foolish because most people will see themselves as the thoroughbred that has made one misstep, and you are just there to put them out of their pain. Once they feel that way, you can use all the logic of Socrates to turn them around. You won't do it. You will not get those people to want to cooperate with you willingly.

It is dangerous because constantly condemning or criticizing or scolding or belittling can injure people mentally, especially your spouse or your kids. It did that to Abraham Lincoln. You have to be very careful.

For a short time, at the very beginning of our years in England, I was guilty of not being very careful. I was under great stress and pressure in my work and my firm, Packages For Semiconductors Co. I didn't have a lot of time to be with my young son, Kyle. I wasn't a very great father at that time. I had fallen into the habit of sometimes being short and grouchy to my son, even when I did get to be with him. Thank God, I had a great wife to cover for me. Then, on one of my trips, this time to an international conference in Rome, Italy to market our products and to sniff-out the latest technological work being done in Eastern and Western Europe, I had one of my "Cold War experiences." Here's what happened -- that time.

It was on a cold, dark, late autumn evening in Rome, Italy that I was snatched off the street and forcibly muscled into a car. They had been able to bait me over to their taxi-looking car because I thought it was the Soviet bloc Polish scientist, Dr. Julian Walenski (whose brain I had been picking at the conference) offering me a lift. But it was not him -- per se, anyway -- and three guys dragged me into the car.

I can still picture the driver. She was an older Italian woman with fiery, crazy-looking eyes, missing and rotten front teeth, and warts all over her face that had thick, black hairs growing from them. She reminded me of Charles Dickens' Madame Defarge, in *A Tale of Two Cities*. The one guy who had an Italian accent was kind of short, broad, and dumpy. The two huge guys wearing overcoats spoke some English, Italian, and an Eastern European language. Their accent sounded like Dr. Julian Walenski's, which is why I was lured over to the car. I knew very well what they were! And we were headed out of Rome.

When we reached the outskirts of Rome, the car stopped to let one of the Eastern European guys out. "That's a break," I said to myself. Now I have only one of the huge guys to contend with. And, though they had frisked me after they muscled me into the back seat of the car, they didn't know that I still had a "weapon". Thank Heaven, and other people, I made sure I always "wore" an innocuous looking weapon for protection when I went on those trips,

I guessed, with great fear, what my ultimate destination was going to be. For, the monster of a man who got out of the car gave the others instructions mentioning Trieste, the notorious passage-city of intrigue and espionage through which people were kidnapped and smuggled to the Communist eastern bloc behind the iron curtain, never again to be seen or heard. When I heard <u>that</u>, I knew I had to make my move.

In the pitch-black darkness of the back seat, under my topcoat, I set up my innocuous weapon -- my beltbuckle-come-brass-knuckles with a spike. When the car stopped for a light, I pulled up on the door-lock, down on the door-handle -- as the big guy who got out had done -- and tried to push open the door to escape. With that, the Eastern European guy grabbed me around the neck. He was not just big. He was strong. When I punched him in the face, the spike of my "beltbuckle" dug into his cheek. He yanked his head back and let go. I pushed on the car door again, but the broad, dumpy Italian guy from the front seat was now outside pushing it closed. The big Eastern European then blind-sided me with a roundhouse punch to the face. The ring of his finger cut me under my eye. He reached inside of his coat to pull out his handgun -- so I had to do it.

(At this point in my telling you this, I have to give you fair warning. If you have a squeamish stomach when it comes to bloodshed, don't read the next paragraph. Skip over it.)

When he went to pull out his handgun, I planted a punch with the spike of my "beltbuckle" right into his left eye. The spike entered into the bottom of his eye-socket. I had to yank hard at it to pull it back out. It must have stuck into bone, or something. As I yanked it out, blood was literally spurting out of his eye as if it were being shot out of one of those paintball guns. He let out with ear-piercing shrieks and screams of pain, the likes of which would strike horror and shock in even the devil. His knee-jerk reaction was to pull his hand from the inside of his overcoat and up to his eye.

Now was my only chance. I immediately pushed the door open to get out. There was no one pushing back this time. The Italian guy and "Madame Defarge" were taking off running down the street. I took off running in the opposite direction.

I eventually came to a well-lit downtown area, immediately flagged-down a <u>real</u> taxi, and jumped right in. I muddled through telling him to take me to Rome. Astonished, he wrote down on a piece of paper how much it would cost. It was a lot. But it was far. And I was desperate. I nodded, okay.

When we finally got to Rome, I checked into a different hotel as a precaution. That night I rested, but could not sleep. I was awake, listening to every little sound.

It was a lurid experience. It gave me pause and perspective. While I was being spirited away by the enemy -- the Eastern Europeans with an accent that sounded like it was Polish or Russian -- my thoughts and fears were not for myself, but that I might never see my wife and little boy again. That was why I would do anything to escape -- and did.

On the airplane back home to England, I kept thinking of how I had sometimes been grouchy and short with my son, always saying to him, don't do this and don't do that. I had by then worked out ways to <u>CORRECT PEOPLE WITHOUT CONDEMNING OR CRITICIZING</u> when it came to my staff at the factory, but I had not really been trying very hard to do that when it came to my son. Sitting in the airplane, a wave of guilt, and shame, and regret came over me. Right then and there I resolved to do something about it.

I didn't waste much time getting to it after I got home. I appropriately explained the cut and shiner under my eye to my wife. Then, later that night, after my son and wife were both sound asleep, I quietly tiptoed into my son's room. I knew there were things that he could not understand if I said them to him, even when awake. Although he was asleep, something nevertheless compelled me to want to talk to him. Like the faith I have that God hears my Confessions, I had faith that God would make my little boy hear and retain in his subconscious mind all the things I was bursting to tell him and was anxious for him to know. I kneeled down on the floor beside his bed and began softly speaking to him.

"Sonny," I whispered, "this time when I was away, I thought I might never see you and Mommy again. I was thinking how I hardly saw you very much because I was always working. And when I did see you, I was usually tired and grouchy and only interested in teaching you a lesson -- always saying, don't do this, or don't do that. I hate the word, don't. I bet you do too.

"I seldom see you like this. You look so peaceful with your little hands and head hugging your favorite little pillow, unaware of the cares and problems of the world.

"I'll never forget the day that I unexpectedly came home to get my wallet, and you were playing in the backyard with your little friends, Paul and Gordon and Stewart. When I heard them get you to ask Mommy for some juice, I almost made you cry right in front of them. I told you they were using you, and you were too easily swayed by them. How dumb I was! You just stood there with your little lower lip quivering, your way of quietly crying inside. I never thought that maybe you were just doing what they do for you at their houses.

"And then there was the time you and I were sitting upstairs in the living room. I was smoking a cigarette and reading my magazine, *Microwaves*. There was a BBC special program on television. It had pictures of how awful the lungs of people looked who have died from cancer because of smoking. Just then, Mommy called from upstairs, telling you it was time to come up to bed. I remember how softly you came over to me to say goodnight, and just stood in front of me with a worried look on your face. I tiredly looked up and grumbled, 'Alright, Kyle, goodnight.' You softly toddled away. Then you stood in the doorway. When I looked up and impatiently asked, 'Well, what is it now?', you just ran back toward me and, with one emotional lunge, threw your arms around me and put your head on my chest and said, 'Oh Daddy. Don't smoke anymore. I don't want you to die!'

"Your little arms hugged me very tightly with a love that only God could have filled your heart with, and that even my stupidity could not dim. Then Mommy called you again, and you went pitter-pattering up our varnished wooden steps.

"And, on the day that I was leaving on this trip, as I was getting into the car to drive to the airport and you were going across Emmanuel Close to your friend Paul's house, you turned around and waved your hand and loudly and enthusiastically shouted out to me, 'Goodbye, Daddy!' Preoccupied with whether I had forgotten anything, I just kind of nodded my head to you and absentmindedly said, 'Okay, goodbye', and drove away without even waving back.

"Little did I know it was almost our last goodbye, Sonny, because one of the nights that I was away on this trip something very terrible happened that made me very, very afraid that I would never see you and Mommy again. So on my way home in the airplane, I thought about how I have not been very careful with what I've been saying to you. Do you know what condemning and criticizing mean? They mean finding fault. And that's what I've been doing to you for your doing little-boy things like just asking Mommy to give you and your friends some juice. That's what I've been doing to you for simply being a good, kind little boy. I've been foolishly expecting you to be something more than just a little boy -- way before you stop being a little boy.

"From now on it's going to be different. Beginning tomorrow, I'm gonna start being a real Daddy to you. We're gonna do lots of things together. When I go for my jog -- my "trotting tour" -- in Brandon Country Park, I'll take you with me. And when you get tired, I'll pick you up and carry you on my shoulders. I'll set up a basketball hoop inside the back of the factory so we can shoot baskets together. And we'll play football and baseball and all those good things. We're gonna hang out together and have fun together.

"I've been trying to treat you as if you were already a grown-up boy. But, as I look at you here in your bed, curled up under the covers, resting from a hard day's playing, your little heart as big and as kind as God can make a heart, I realize it was only yesterday that you were a baby in your Mom's arms, hugging her, your little head nestled into her shoulder. I know you'll be a good, kind grown-up someday, but right now, you are still only a little boy. I have expected too much from you. I've been too demanding. I have not been careful."

From then on, I <u>was</u> careful. I did all the things I told my son I would do that night when he was asleep. If he needed to be corrected for some good reason, I was careful to use the Rule that I had been applying to my employees: <u>CORRECT PEOPLE WITHOUT CONDEMNING OR CRITICIZING</u>. For instance, if by chance he allowed those twin mental cancers, idleness and boredom, to corrode his happiness, I would keep in mind, CALL ATTENTION TO PEOPLE'S MISTAKES INDIRECTLY, and tell him something like, "People get famous because they practice every minute they have a chance, Kyle." He would lift himself up and go to the back of the factory and shoot baskets or practice throwing his green rubber ball at a target I drew on the factory wall. Or, when he made the mistake of thinking I would be angry because he was too tired to go further when we were doing what we called our trotting-tour -- our jog -- in Brandon Country Park, I would call on, MAKE PEOPLE'S MISTAKES SEEM EASY TO CORRECT, by simply picking him up and jogging with him on my shoulders. He was <u>so</u> happy. He would kind of giggle. He loved it. And I never again criticized him in front of his friends. I would call on, LET PEOPLE SAVE FACE, and correct him later. When I did that, I would try to FIRST TALK ABOUT MISTAKES <u>I</u> HAVE MADE, like smoking. And, by the way, I <u>did</u> stop smoking.

If you want to correct someone, or change someone, or improve someone -- a colleague, a family member, someone you are the leader of, someone who is the leader of you -- sometimes there is someone else you have to begin with first. Do you know who that is? It's you, yourself -- as it was with me. And remember this: condemning and criticizing is like a spark that can ignite and explode open an otherwise dormant and harmless powder keg of raw emotions, resentment, and intentional non-cooperation. Any fool can stand there and find fault and condemn and criticize. And, it is a fool who usually does. If you want to be a great real-life leader, however, you have to be understanding and insightful enough to figure out why people do what they do, and find good ways to CORRECT PEOPLE WITHOUT CONDEMNING OR CRITICIZING. If even God does not judge people until the end of their days, why should we presume that we are qualified to do so?

Robert E. Lee and Ulysses S. Grant and Abraham Lincoln and, eventually, even I knew that, of all the cocktails ever conjured up by Satan in the fiery cauldrons of hell, the cocktail of condemning - criticizing - nagging - belittling is the most deadly one. It's like a cocktail of arsenic. As a cocktail of arsenic never fails to kill humans and animals, this cocktail never fails to kill human relations and leadership.

And so, as actions speak louder than words, I ask that you start today to put one of the best bits of sage advice ever given about the fine art of leadership into action, which is our:

KEY # 2: CORRECT PEOPLE WITHOUT CONDEMNING OR CRITICIZING

And you can do that in one or all of these four ways:

1.) - CALL ATTENTION TO PEOPLE'S MISTAKES INDIRECTLY.

2.) - MAKE PEOPLE'S MISTAKES SEEM EASY TO CORRECT.

3.) - LET PEOPLE SAVE FACE.

4.) - FIRST TALK ABOUT MISTAKES YOU HAVE MADE.

Chapter 4: Do This ... It's What Everyone Wants

"One morning (I am now quoting my own words), years ago, like a shot out of the dark, my Dad's doctor told him he had acute granulocytic leukemia, and only a few months to live. Life suddenly became confused and out of control.

"During those last few months of his life at their retirement home in the Holiday City section of Toms River, New Jersey, I spent more time talking to him than ever before.

"Surprisingly, though Dad had always been content to be a quiet listener, he now did a lot of the talking. He talked about growing up in western Pennsylvania, about his Mom and Dad, about playing high school sports, and about working in the steel mill before World War II. He talked about his fighting in the Pacific during World War II, something he had never before wanted to talk about. I just listened in awe. He told me that his 'outfit', the 77th Infantry Division, was called 'the Marine's Army division' because they fought together so often. He told me about his Silver Stars, about the guys in his outfit whose lives he had saved, about guys who died, about 'returning' to the Phillipines with MacArthur, about the battles leading to their invasion of Okinawa, Japan, about his battlefield Commission to Lieutenant. He showed me the awards and commendations he received later in life from the US Postal Service. He talked about his and Mom's financial position -- tax returns and so on that he always handled. I answered, 'of course', when he said to me, 'Promise to help your Mom to handle all of that when I am no longer here.' He talked a lot about golf: teaching Mom to play; playing golf with us boys; his golf trophies.

"During those weeks, I listened to everything he wanted to tell me. Strangely enough, for the first time that I can ever remember, it seemed necessary to him to feel important. He wanted me to feel that he was important. In the end, I guess everyone wants to feel that their time upon this stage called Life was important in some way."

"One day, close to the end, Dad began to talk about <u>me</u>. We talked about my work. He asked me about my college days at Rutgers. We talked about my football and baseball playing days. He told me how proud he and Mom were of my degree in engineering. Then, like a bolt from the blue, he asked, 'Why is it you never invited your Mom and me to graduation from Rutgers?' He said that he can remember how the folks at Rutgers had forewarned Mom and him that during those days of huge demand and few engineering spaces, only about half who started would end up getting through Rutgers College of Engineering. They had been so much looking forward to seeing their son be one of the half who got through.

"His look of disappointment was a killer. It really hurt. It stopped my heart for a few seconds. For, I would never want to cause Mom or Dad to be hurt in any way. I believe that they would measure up to Plato's description of the ideal mother and father. So reluctantly, I lifted (slightly) my veil of secrecy for him and told him some things, knowing he would take them to the grave with him. And I told him that I also felt, at the time, that graduation exercises were only an unimportant formality anyway. Now I feel differently. I had never thought during all those years, however, that it meant so much to Mom and Dad. I felt ashamed of myself. I realized way too late that I had let them down.

"During his very last hours here on this Earth, when I was at his bedside, I kept thinking about what a good man he was to have married Mom at the end of World War II with three kids in tow, and what a good Dad he had been during all these years. It struck me that I had always taken the time to confide in him as my Dad, but I had never taken the time to confide in him as my friend. It hit me hard that I had been so indifferent, and that I had lost the chance to make him a special friend -- a special kind of buddy. It struck me, too late, that he had always wanted to be the friend and buddy of my brothers and me. Oh, how I missed out, I thought to myself. I could not hold back my tears.

"He told me how much he loved us boys. I realized that I could not remember whether I had ever said, 'I love you, Dad.' I told him, 'I love you, Dad'.

"To me, Dad clearly proved that 'nurture' is far more important than 'nature'. It hadn't even occurred to me that, when I didn't invite them to my college graduation exercises, it had made him feel that he was not important in my life. For, he <u>was</u> important. Again, it was partly what I had to do, and partly my youthful immaturity.

" Now that Dad is no longer with us, it's too late for me to redeem my youthful mistakes and shortcomings as far as he is concerned. But when we received the West Point announcement about our son Kyle's graduation, I made sure I first and foremost invited Mom -- sitting here -- to come to the graduation exercises, as well as, to be our guest, as are all of you, for this dinner celebration. As an Army hero in WWII, I know Dad would have been especially proud of Kyle. How I wish I could have made up for <u>my</u> graduation, and could have invited him to be here today with all of us. Now it's too late.

"But who knows. Could it be? Maybe he <u>is</u> here with us -- in another way? Though I know he can't come back, mortally, across the one-way threshold between worlds, through the non-return valve of Eternity, perhaps God has allowed him to come back in some other way, spiritually. So, if we do have an invisible guest with us here today, I want him to know, and all of you to know, that he is important to me .... and I invited him. And this is his seat -- right here -- between Mom and me."

What I just quoted above is about one half of a speech I had written and intended to give at my son Kyle's graduation dinner at West Point's Thayer Hotel. I never gave it. When the time came, I was too choked-up to deliver it. I failed. And I didn't want anyone to know that I failed. I never told a living soul. I didn't think it necessary to do so. I was too proud and too embarrassed to admit I couldn't do it. No, not a <u>living</u> soul ever heard that speech. But -- I believe my Dad did!

The reason that I revealed these long held secrets of mine to you is to drive home a powerful message: Everyone wants to feel important. Think about it. You don't have to be a brilliant, world-renowned psychologist to figure it out. If you have the genuine desire to be a great real-life leader -- a leader who can get people to <u>want</u> to follow you and cooperate with you <u>willingly and voluntarily</u> -- one of the things you can do is evoke the magic of our:

<u>KEY # 3: MAKE PEOPLE FEEL IMPORTANT</u>

I never thought of this at the time, but some time later it occurred to me that, during those last days with my Dad, I had made him feel important merely by letting him do most of the talking while I was being a good listener. And it struck me that, all of his life, his being content to be a quiet, humble, good listener helped me by making <u>me</u> feel important. So, one of the ways to **MAKE PEOPLE FEEL IMPORTANT** is:

1.) – BE A GOOD LISTENER (let people talk about themselves)

Everyone you meet -- even the person you see in the mirror -- wants to feel important. Here is a really, really astonishing, historically-true story that is a powerful example of the fine leadership art of making people feel important by being a good listener.

In 1944, during World War II, General George S. Patton poignantly said, "God, deliver us from our friends ... we can handle the enemy." Lucky for us, and unlucky for Adolf Hitler's army of the Third German Reich, Supreme Allied Commander Dwight D. Eisenhower was sympathetic to Patton and his views. When Patton was figuratively being slapped-down for literally having slapped-down two American soldiers to bring them to their senses -- convinced they had merely given-in to their worries and anxieties about the battlefield and getting killed -- Eisenhower sympathetically listened to Patton's philosophical explanation for his remedial actions. He bought into Patton's self-defense, for he had seen the same kind of battlefield anxiety himself. Then he moved on to talk about Patton's military qualities. He heartened a General George S. Patton whose stock was down because of the slapping incidents by telling him that he had been of incalculable value in the War thus far, and assured him that he was indispensable to victory.

Though Patton was despondent for having been put on the shelf over the slapping incidents, Eisenhower -- "Ike" -- further lifted his spirits and continued to make him feel important by telling him that his military qualities were magnificent -- "close to the best of our classic examples," that he had a "native shrewdness about logistics," and that he was "a truly aggressive commander with brains." And that set the stage for one of the most astute military deceptions ever to be used in the history of warfare, without which the Allies might not have been able to successfully pull off the Normandy Invasion.

Adolf Hitler knew the allies were undergoing a massive buildup in England in preparation for some sort of major invasion of Europe (which by then had been almost completely conquered by Hitler's armies), but did not know when or where. That's where Patton came in. There was enormous respect for, and fear of, Patton among the German high staff. They considered him to be the Allies' best general. There is no way, they concluded, that anyone other than the Allies' best general would lead an invasion into Europe. Therefore, Eisenhower, Patton, and the Allies concocted an enormous deception to fool Hitler by creating a bogus headquarters, phony camps, and dummy war equipment made from inflatibles, cardboard, etc.. They fudged radio traffic and did bogus air surveillance to allow Hitler to "figure out" that the invasion would be across the narrow part of the English Channel at Calais, by Patton. Hitler "cleverly" repositioned his powerful 15th Army at that point to give Patton the surprise reception of his life. But, as we know, the surprise was on him. The real invasion took place along the beaches of Normandy, further south.

Though our invasion was ultimately successful, the resistance of Hitler's defenses at Normandy turned out to be devastating due to General Erwin Rommel's phenomenal fortifications. You can imagine what it would have been like if Hitler's entire 15th Army had also been there. The invasion almost certainly would have been crushed, with horrendous loss of American, British, and Canadian life.

The success of the entire operation, code-named Operation Overlord, was made possible because Ike's great real-life leadership turned Patton around. Ike convinced Patton that he was still so important that he was the only one who could pull off the deception of Operation Overlord. He got Patton, who dreamed of leading the real invasion, to cooperate -- and not grudgingly, but willingly.

General Eisenhower saved tens of thousands of lives employing fine leadership art by deciding to BE A GOOD LISTENER (let people talk about themselves) in order to <u>MAKE PEOPLE FEEL IMPORTANT</u>. In this case, "people" was General Patton who had been in hot water, suffering from crippling condemnation by a presumptive American press, and feeling rejected and perhaps not indispensable to victory after all.

As a postscript, it's now history that, after Operation Overlord, Patton went on to roll up Hitler's formidable armies in one challenge after the other. Although he was not loved by everyone because his style of leadership, true to what he had learned at West Point, was to be tough-but-caring, his style of war-making struck fear into the hearts of Hitler's generals who continued to call him the Allies' best Field General. That was the Patton "<u>tri</u>chotomy". He was respected, hated, and loved, all at the same time.

Speaking of love, do you guys who are reading this book want to know how to make a gal fall in love with you? You'll like this because it's easy -- works like a charm. Far be it from little-ole-me, however, to have unearthed the big secret. I'm even lucky I got my wife to fall in love with me! But wait 'til you hear who <u>did</u> tell me the secret. Believe it or not, I got it straight from the lips of -- Rex Harrison; yes, the famous English star of "My Fair Lady" -- Rex Harrison. Here's how that came about.

During my years in England, on one of my flights from London to New York, I was upgraded to first class on the Boeing 747 -- the one with the second-floor lounge. When we were in the air and allowed to unbuckle, I decided to go up to the second-floor lounge to do some reading. When I got there, a man and woman together were the only other ones there. As I sat down on the couch opposite them, the man looked up, gave a little smile, and said hello. After I did a double take, I realized it was Rex Harrison. I introduced myself. He followed by introducing himself and his wife -- his sixth wife. We exchanged small talk for a while; then the conversation gradually got around to talking about marriage. When I asked him what was his trick to getting all those beautiful women, like his present wife, to fall in love with him, he said, "It's no trick uh-tall. I sha'nt bore you with a personal secret about myself that few know about, but I shall tell you that, as a young man, reared in a small village in the northeast of England near Liverpool, a tragedy of my youth that I had to overcome made me very self-conscious about myself.

"I was so self-conscious that, in conversation with young ladies, I would do very little, if any, of the talking to avoid looking them straight in the eye. I would get them to do the talking by asking questions that would make them tell me about themselves -- you know, their hobbies, their interests, their experiences, their aspirations for the future. When I did that, a curious thing happened. The more they talked about themselves, the more I found them becoming interested in <u>me</u>, and I sometimes found I completely forgot about my self-consciousness. I actually found myself becoming really quite popular with the ladies when I did that. So, you see, there's no trick to it uh-tall. You simply find what it is interests them. Then become a good listener and let them talk about themselves."

Nothing is so interesting to "Jane" as …….. "Jane". I don't think you have to study at Oxford or Cambridge to know, when "Jane" looks at a group photograph that she is in, she looks for her own face first. It's the same deal with anyone, woman or man. Most people are twenty times more interested in themselves than in you. Therefore, the magic road to a woman's heart is to start talking about her, a subject she treasures most.

And so, you guys, if there is an object of your affection out there, make her interested in you by being interested in her. Then, be a good listener. By the way, the same idea works for you gals reading this book who would like to get that man of your dreams to propose marriage to you. Generally speaking, it works for anyone who simply wants to win someone's heart, or for anyone who has a leadership interest in making other people want to cooperate willingly and voluntarily. If you will simply BE A GOOD LISTENER (let people talk about themselves), you will magically MAKE PEOPLE FEEL IMPORTANT.

I highly doubt that you could scare up very many fine souls this side of Heaven to use as proof that people do not have a sincere desire to feel important. I also doubt that you could count on many from up There, or down here, who are proof against their own name having been, or being, the most important word in any language to them. Most people are more interested in their own name than all the names in Heaven, or on Earth. Not only does "Jane" or "John" first look for their own face in a group picture, they also first look for their own name in the caption below the picture. Even Andrew Carnegie, America's richest and most successful steel industry tycoon, appreciated the immense importance people place in their own names.

My Dad, his brother (Uncle Chuck), and their father (a grand-dad I never knew) actually worked in one of the steel mills originally founded by Andrew Carnegie. Uncle Chuck, who worked his way up the ladder of success to be the Superintendent (top dog) of his mill, passed a story on to me that had been passed down to them by his dad. Here it is, as he told it to me.

Andrew Carnegie was a people person who frequently visited all of his steel mills. When he did so, he didn't just stop by to say hello to "Mike the manager". He spent time on the shop floor with "Tom, Dick, and Harry." He made a special effort to chat with, and know the names of his shop floor workers. They were proud that they were on a first name basis with the big, big, big boss.

One time, a few rabble-rousers in my grand-dad's mill tried to get the workers to go on strike. The workers overwhelmingly voted the initiative down. And what was their reason? They said, "We know and like 'Andrew' personally -- he is our friend -- and we're not about to stab him in the back."

Andrew Carnegie's honoring the names of his workers and business contacts was one of the secrets of his success. Though he was dubbed "The Steel King," he was not at all a genius at metallurgy and engineering. But he did have a genius for leadership. He possessed a natural sense of how important it is to <u>MAKE PEOPLE FEEL IMPORTANT</u>. And he knew that one of the ways to do that was to:

2.) - MAKE PEOPLE'S NAMES IMPORTANT

Only half the lure of Hollywood and television is big money. The other half is fame. It's the feeling of importance people get from name recognition -- having their name up in lights, or on the big silver screen, or on millions of television screens.

Did you know that before electricity gave us radio, television, and the movies, rich people would actually pay a load of money to authors if they would dedicate their books to them? They wanted their names to be a permanent record for posterity. And that's also why many museums, libraries, and other cultural venues bear the names of rich people who blanched at the thought that their precious names might perish from this Earth, rather than live on in the memory of mankind. Rich people have poured-out millions of dollars to be honored with making their names important. But, I'm not saying there cannot also be noble philanthropic reasons involved.

For example, do you know how prestigious Duke University got its name back in 1934? James Duke, the cigarette tycoon, offered forty million dollars (imagine how much that is today) to Trinity College in North Carolina if the college would change its name to Duke University in honor of him, so that his name would live on in posterity. As we know, Trinity College accepted the offer. But that's not unusual. Yale, Harvard, Rutgers, Stanford, Rice and many other colleges got their names that way.

Some people are honored and made to feel important by having something named after them because of their good deeds, not just because of money. We have all seen buildings and roads named after people for that reason. Yes, everyone knows that's not an unusual way to MAKE PEOPLE'S NAMES IMPORTANT.

Now let me tell you about what is an unusual way, what West Point does, to MAKE PEOPLE'S NAMES IMPORTANT.

In the early years of West Point -- the United States Military Academy -- beginning back in the early 1800's, new cadets, 'Plebes', were intentionally deprived of wearing a nameplate on their uniforms. Sporting their names would make them feel important, and that's the last thing that West Point wanted to do. Plebes were supposed to start out as the most unimportant wretches on earth and gradually earn their recognition. They were called every imaginative name in the book other than their real names. Only after they scratched and clawed their way back up from the abyss of Plebe year to earn their rite of passage would they be called by their real names.

During more recent decades, West Point has allowed Plebes to wear nameplates for easier identification because the sheer number of plebes has grown so large. However, upper-class cadets still do not refer to Plebes by their first names, often employing the "creative-name" tradition. For West Point still begins its training regimen by wrecking the dream ships of overconfident high school graduates on the sharp coral reefs of humility. Then, finally, the blue skies and sunshine and fabulous port called "Recognition" finally comes into sight. They race toward it with pride, with the wind at their backs, with the wind whistling through their masts, with the wind puffing-out their sails. When they reach that fabulous port on that seemingly magical day called Recognition Day, upper-class cadets for the first time call Plebes by their names. After many hard months out at sea, Recognized Plebes are welcomed home and made to feel important. The upper-class cadets shake their hands, introduce themselves, use first and last names, and initiate a normal wholesome chain-of-command leadership relationship based on respect. The Recognized Plebes have now earned their badges of individuality. They finally have their names back. And, how special their names now sound!

The point I am making here is: Though in an inverted and unusual way, even West Point uses MAKE PEOPLE'S NAMES IMPORTANT in its otherwise focused aim at installing the virtuous software program of duty-honor-country (which actually amounts to character-morals-ethics) into the hard drive of its cadets' minds.

Belonging in the leadership league of West Point and renowned leaders like Alexander the Great, Julius Caesar, George Washington, Napoleon Bonaparte, Abraham Lincoln, Winston Churchill, Franklin Roosevelt, Ronald Reagan, and others who are among the greatest real-life leaders of all time, there is also none other than -- Paul of Tarsus.

Are you asking, Paul who? What did he do? Who is he? Well, back around 47 AD, Paul of Tarsus did no less than blend the good parts of Hammurabi's Laws, Akenhaten's One God, Moses' Laws, and the Judaic Testaments with the teachings of Jesus the Christ, and, adding just the right flavoring of Greek philosophy (especially Plato's), he cooked up this new fangled religious philosophy that he called -- Christianity. (For a concise overview of the above, see my book, *Understanding West Point, Leaders of Character, and Thomas Jefferson*). I call it religious philosophy because philosophy means "love of knowledge," and

Paul of Tarsus did more than travel around to sell the <u>belief</u> that Jesus is the son of God. He also told people about his own first-hand witnessing -- therefore, first-hand <u>knowledge</u> -- of the miracles and teachings of Jesus here on Earth; of his first-hand witnessing of Jesus coming back after being dead; and, of his first-hand witnessing, right before his and others' eyes, of Jesus rising up into the sky and disappearing. Yes, disappearing! To where? God only knows. But believers call it Heaven.

Paul of Tarsus, who the world now knows as St. Paul, was no simple, gullible guy. He was an educated Pharisee with a gilded tongue and philosophical penchant. He actually began as an enemy of Jesus and his disciples; he had been responsible for persecuting and prosecuting people in Jesus' movement. As he heard Jesus' disciples explaining their religious thoughts to defend themselves against persecution, he himself began to believe what they were saying. It was contagious. Then one night he had a divine epiphany that turned him into an advocate of Jesus' teachings. He too became a follower of Jesus.

While out on the evangelizing trail around the Mediterranean, because his reputation by then preceded him wherever he went, he was on one occasion being afforded great esteem by the people of Athens, Greece. Out of jealously, some Stoic and Epicurean philosophers, and prominent politicians intentionally tried to embarrass and belittle him before crowds of people. They stood him up, laughed at him, and said, "What will this babbler say?" They then escorted him to the Areopagus, the ancient, low-lying hill next to the Acropolis where court was held and witnesses were heard. There he stood on the crest of Mars Hill of the famous Areopagus in front of what now had grown into a huge crowd of people (perhaps thousands) looking up at him, expecting him to "babble" endlessly about this new thing regarding some strange new god. How could he neutralize their natural belligerence and make them want to listen to him and <u>want</u> to follow the Christian doctrine, <u>willingly</u>?

He began by asking the philosophers and prominent Athenians their opinions on why he is there and what they are expecting, saying he held their opinions in high esteem, to which they replied:

"May we know what this new doctrine, whereof thou speakest, is? For thou bringest certain strange things to our ears; we would know therefore what these things mean." (See *The Bible*, Acts of the Apostles, 17: 17-34.)

With that, he suspected the city fathers were about to subtly trump up bogus charges against him, as were long ago trumped up against Socrates, because what he was about to say could be easily interpreted as a threat to their high positions of importance in Athens. Then he came up with a brilliant idea, perhaps divinely revealed.

On the way in , he had passed by many statues, shrines, temples, and altars to their many different gods. He remembered that there was one prominent altar with the markings: TO THE UNKNOWN GOD. So he began his sermon by saying:

"Ye men of Athens ..... as I passed by, and beheld your devotions, I found an altar with this inscription: TO THE UNKNOWN GOD ..... Him declare I unto you." (See *The Bible*, Acts of the Apostles, 17: 17-34).

In other words, he was telling them, "Athenians have had the idea of there being an Unknown God long before Christianity came along. So, your idea is finally now confirmed. The idea is really yours. I, Paul, am just here to tell you all about your Unknown God, as told to me firsthand by the Son of your Unknown God, Jesus the Christ."

Far from being a threat to the philosophers and prominent Athenians, St. Paul made them even more important in their fellow countrymen's eyes by his holding their opinions in high esteem and handing to them much of the credit for the idea of Christianity.

St. Paul's immortal sermon in Athens is one of the most brilliant examples of great real-life leadership by, arguably, the greatest leader of all time. He's the greatest leader of all time? St. Paul? Yes, indeed. Just think about it. Paul did not have Jesus' divinity. He had no armies. He was not a king, not a ruler, not a president. He had only a cause -- a cause that was greater than himself. But he got people to <u>want</u> to follow that cause <u>willingly and voluntarily</u>. In 47 AD Athens, he got many thousands to follow willingly. Millions around the world began to follow. Eventually, hundreds of millions followed willingly.

St. Paul's fielding the adversity of Athenians is a beautiful example of our leadership <u>KEY # 3: MAKE PEOPLE FEEL IMPORTANT</u>. And the way he made them feel important was to:

3.) – LET OTHER PEOPLE FEEL THE IDEA IS THEIRS

Thomas Jefferson did the same thing as St. Paul. I don't mean he went around evangelizing for Christianity. Like St. Paul, he had a cause that was greater than himself, however. And he got people to follow that cause willingly.

You're probably thinking to yourself, "I know. He's talking about the Declaration of Independence, or the Louisiana Purchase". Well, in fact, I'm not. I'm talking about the little-known, never told story of his having done no less than save America! That's right. I said, "Save America, and save our democratic republic!" You probably never learned that in school, so here's the story of how he did it that you can tell other people.

Jefferson was the last living leader of a painful and turbulent American revolutionary period, along with John Adams. In spite of that generation's winning independence from England, did you know that to his dying day, Thomas Jefferson felt that they had not yet completely finished the Revolution? Why? Because he felt that "representative government", as we still have today, was only "a good first start". The people had been led to believe that they would have what he wanted to have -- true direct participatory democracy for a <u>provenly informed</u> citizenry. To him, the shooting was over, but it was still an unfinished revolution.

Before he came to the Presidency he had three goals, three visions for America.

His first goal was, through reforming government, halt the country's rapid slide back to the British style of monarchy that many powerful people still wanted.

His second goal was, find a way to preserve, protect, and defend the country and the Constitution against all foreign and domestic threats, <u>permanently</u> -- for all time.

His third goal was, finally give the people true direct participatory democracy.

Jefferson would never see this third goal of true direct participatory democracy come about. But he made sure that future generations would have a shot at it. To do that, he had to successfully pull off his first and second goals: halt the march of monarchism; permanently preserve, protect, and defend the fledgling new nation. Here's the way great real-life leadership accomplished those two goals.

England and all of Europe always considered American democracy in a republic after the Revolutionary War as little more than a tenuous experiment. President George Washington was able to preserve, protect, and defend the "experiment" because of his towering image and the respect he commanded all over America and Europe. When he died, Europeans figured the experiment would finally die with him. They were ready to pounce on us and carve the country up among themselves again.

Thomas Jefferson surprised them all. He reformed the country with his "chaste reformation" (meaning, non-violent), and went about protecting and defending the country by creating two new, unique institutions: West Point; and, a "good" standing army.

West Point was to produce army officers who are leaders of character having Virtue and knowledge, a new way of assuring the loyalty of, and removing the fear of, a standing army …. unlike standing armies throughout history that were pawns of a king or dictator, or always a threat to overthrow their government. The new kind of American "good" standing army would be Jefferson's <u>permanent</u> solution to the problem of how to preserve, protect, and defend our way of life and our Constitution. America would never again have to tenuously depend on someone's towering reputation and image to do that. The American "experiment" would finally be changed from experiment to fact. And, if not achieved in Jefferson's lifetime, future generations could have a shot at true direct participatory democracy for its informed citizens.

Thomas Jefferson always thought that the University of Virginia, his lifelong, high-profile, high budget pet project would come along in time to get a feather in its cap for helping him to save America. It didn't. But West Point, his secret, low profile, low budget project, did. He lived to see West Point fulfill his dream of constantly renewing the spirit of 1776, of making the young understand the daunting feat accomplished by the departed Revolutionary generation, and of allowing future generations to continue what their forefathers began. He saw his West Point turn into an institution truly bridging past and present.

Historians were never able to treat Thomas Jefferson's saving America through his chaste reformation that created West Point and a West Point-led, good standing army as a "cause-celebre" because of the chaste, subtle, secret way he had to do it. However, his doing so is one of the most wonderful examples of great real-life leadership in American history. And, although West Point probably played the single most important role in saving America, he could never take credit for the founding of West Point. He had to be content to LET OTHER PEOPLE FEEL THE IDEA IS THEIRS. I know. That calls for another, "Why?". Here's why.

Proposals for a military academy had been crushed on numerous occasions because of the historic fears of a standing army. Jefferson himself even came out against it as George Washington's Secretary of State when Washington proposed one. No less than fourteen different people had unsuccessful proposals for a military academy at one time or another. Then Thomas Jefferson once again showed why he richly deserves to be called America's philosophical father when he came up with the philosophical idea of how the country could safely have a military academy and how to get the idea passed by a Congress that previously killed every single military academy proposal by a wide margin. That included his resolving to remain the secret prime mover behind the founding of West Point by deciding to LET OTHER PEOPLE FEEL THE IDEA IS THEIRS, as long as it got done.

As we know, it did get done, and his secret involvement behind the scenes was well kept. In fact, when money was raised for a Thomas Jefferson stone monument, merely because West Point surfaced during his watch as president, the project was dead on arrival because he was not credited with having been the founder. Only an oil painting was commissioned. And that remained the sole nexus of West Point to Jefferson for nearly two hundred years -- until the history-making breakthrough that took several years of research that was officially recorded and copyrighted in 1998 and made into a book that revealed the real story of West Point and Thomas Jefferson (Remick, Norman Thomas. *Mr. Jefferson's Academy: The Real Story Behind West Point*. NJ: RPR, 1999. And its successor issues).

After that book in 1999, everyone jumped on board. The West Point-Jefferson bandwagon began to fill up. And Jefferson finally got his due recognition. This time when money was raised for a "monument" -- for a West Point memorial to Thomas Jefferson -- it was not quashed by Congress, or others. The stone monument this time became a reality, the new Thomas Jefferson Library at West Point.

The point of this short history lesson about how Thomas Jefferson saved America is this: As Jefferson had to keep from waving his own flag by keeping his true involvement a secret in order to establish West Point, sometimes you too will have to do the same to get cooperation and results. So, if you are more interested in results than in who gets the credit, then sometimes you have to: LET OTHER PEOPLE FEEL THE IDEA IS THEIRS.

Leaving aside food, sleep, and a few of the other <u>physical</u> cravings of human nature, one of the strongest human cravings is the desire to have respect. That's what drove Charles Dickens and other immortal authors to write their timeless novels. It's what inspired giants of industry like Andrew Carnegie, John D. Rockefeller, and Bill Gates to be entrepreneurs.

The hunger that people have for money is not just to wallow in it, become fat and happy, and bask in luxuries. Having a ton of money and being able to flaunt and enjoy the material things of life also satisfies the human hunger and thirst for respect. Isn't that why some people you know build houses that are much bigger than they can use, God bless them, and those houses are in a way really their own monuments to themselves, being much larger than even luxurious living demands? How many rich blessed ones have you seen lately who <u>do not</u> ostentatiously flaunt their own possessions in public for everyone to see? Why do you reckon they do that? They do that because it makes them feel respected.

The unvarnished truth is that everyone can't be respected because they're rich, because everyone can't be rich. But everyone you meet today, tomorrow, and every day, be they butcher, baker, or hamburger maker, not only has a natural longing and yearning to be respected, but has some God-given ability or characteristic that <u>should</u> be respected. Since the beginning of time, philosophers like Socrates, poets like Emerson, statesman like Lincoln, and most importantly, Jesus Christ himself have said in so many words, "Every person is in some way your superior." Remember that simple refrain the next time you feel the hoity-toity to look down your nose at someone.

A long time ago in the Dutch West Indies, a boy of fourteen, who hoity-toity people of those islands were already looking down their noses at, was struggling just to exist after a series of tragedies left him homeless. His unmarried mother had died, he had no father, his older cousin who was supposed to be his guardian committed a very bloody suicide, and his aunt, uncle, and grandmother had all previously died within a short time span of each other. Already feeling the sting and humiliation and disrespect of being called one of the many fatherless "bastards" on his slave-laden, sugar-growing, West Indies island on which he was born and still lived, he was now friendless and penniless and stripped of any notion that life is fair.

It was in this state of desperation that the youth finally landed a job with a mercantile house in St. Croix. It didn't take long for him to climb up the ladder a few rungs by demonstrating the ability to clearly and precisely keep track of the sugar and dry goods and building materials and other commodities the company traded. He was also able to write in such a clear and flowing style that he was encouraged to submit written articles to the local bilingual newspaper, *The Royal Gazette*.

Then the islands were hit by a devastating hurricane. He decided to write an article for the *Gazette* that meticulously described the hurricane and called it: "The Most Disastrous Hurricane Known to the Memory of Man." The disrespected, young "bastard" didn't know it at the time, but he had just written his ticket out of poverty and off the island. For, once his verbal well-water began to rise to the surface, it became a freely flowing fountain of words that began to attract all kinds of attention.

The hurricane had driven home the fact that St. Croix had an abiding need for doctors, and not for just after hurricanes, but to treat the tropical diseases that constantly plagued the islands. Consequently, a group of merchants and other businessmen got together and sponsored a fund to send promising youth, which included him, to North America for an education, hopefully to qualify for studying medicine.

That was the turning point of his life. When he landed in North America, he could now tuck his disastrous boyhood skeletons away in a closet and never open the door again. He could cut himself off from his past and become acquitted for what he did, and not be condemned for what he was.

Armed with letters of introduction that gave no hint of his illegitimacy, he threw off the pox of being known as a "bastard" that had haunted his entire youth. And, profiting from the respect he was given at his school in Elizabeth, New Jersey, and inspired by the respect he received at Kings College in New York City (now, Columbia U.), he went on to make a name for himself in history that became emblazoned across the skies of America during and after the Revolutionary War. I think you've heard of this young man. His name was Alexander Hamilton.

History is well stocked with stories of how the pure magic of giving someone respect has electrified their willingness to cooperate and make a cause or mission successful, like this one about Alexander Hamilton. When you show "John" and "Jenny" authentic respect, it's like leading them to a spring of water when they're dying of thirst crossing Death Valley, California. They will forever more think, "Now I know who I'm going to follow." Are they going to follow someone who doesn't make them feel good and show them respect? I'll let you answer that.

Therefore, the fourth way for you to <u>MAKE PEOPLE FEEL IMPORTANT</u> so that they <u>willingly and voluntarily want</u> you as their leader is to satisfy their natural thirst for respect by showing that you respect them for some ability, or character trait, or something they do. So be sure to:

4.) – LET PEOPLE KNOW YOU RESPECT THEM

If you want to brighten the lights and oil the wheels of your vehicle to great real-life leadership, begin to implement the important, but very simple, philosophy you have learned in this chapter. And you don't have to wait until you're elected to the House of Representatives or elected the president of your local Little League to do it. When should you begin? How does, right now, sound? Where? The answer is, anywhere you are. How? As this chapter is easy to put into action immediately, the answer is, use:

KEY #3: MAKE PEOPLE FEEL IMPORTANT

And implement it in any or all of our four ways:

1.) – BE A GOOD LISTENER (let people talk about themselves).

2.) – MAKE PEOPLE'S NAMES IMPORTANT.

3.) – LET OTHER PEOPLE FEEL THE IDEA IS THEIRS.

4.) – LET PEOPLE KNOW YOU RESPECT THEM.

Chapter 5: Do This ... It's An Appeal That Everyone Loves

When I was a young lad of twelve years old growing up in Paterson, N. J., a real miracle saved me from being murdered in broad daylight!

I lived in a racially all-white village of very small Cape Cod houses at the base of the wooded, undeveloped, Preakness Mountains, called Colonial Village. After the Second World War, the government built "The Projects" right next to Colonial Village. They were hundreds of welfare/low income row houses, racially mostly black. The white kids from the Village and the black kids from the Projects played baseball, basketball, and tackle football against each other. Eventually, we got to choosing up sides by "chugging up" on a bat or "shooting" fingers to pick sides according to how good you were instead of what color you were.

This one time, some of our black friends whose families had moved to the Projects to escape the notorious crime-ridden slums of Paterson called the River Street Section, were challenged by their former River Street friends to a regular football game.

When the day for the game arrived, we all showed up -- both Projects and Village kids because that was our team -- at the dirt parking lot of Paterson's renowned Hincliffe Stadium where both sides agreed to play the game because we didn't have a regular field in those days. The River Street kids were shocked to see white kids on the team. They didn't like that I was the quarterback and that half the team was white kids. This was the 1950's.

They especially didn't like it when the game was over, and we had slaughtered them, even though Clarence Smith, "Smitty", our fastest kid, and William Williams, "Willie", our biggest kid, who had combined to run or catch passes for all ten of our touchdowns, were both black kids from the Projects.

There were a few adults who acted as referees for the game, more to prevent fights than to make sure we stuck to the rules. When they left, little did I know that an older non-player from River Street, maybe sixteen years old, stole up to me from behind for some unknown reason with a thick steel chain. He swung the chain at me from behind, and the next thing I knew, it had twirled tightly around my neck a couple of turns. He then yanked me down to the ground and began to drag me around like a dog.

I was choking. I couldn't breathe. I can remember getting terrified because I was losing consciousness. I was sure at that moment that I was about to die.

The River Street kids were all standing on one side laughing. Willie and Smitty and one other kid were the only ones left there from our team. With what had to be my last breath of air, I looked up at my friends Willie and Smitty and barely gasped the words, "Help me". With that, I faintly remember them looking at each other, then jumping on the older, bigger thug, breaking his hold on the chain, and wrestling him to the ground.

When I came-to again, the chain was gone and all the River Street kids were gone. Only Willie and Smitty were there. I was so happy to be alive and breathing. They had saved my life. I never told anyone at home because I wanted to continue playing football.

When I was choking and gasped out to Willie and Smitty to help me, I saw that it aroused something deep inside of them -- their natural, God-given pride and emotions. I think that everyone alive has pride, emotions, and a high regard for their own goodness. All of us, be we baker, banker, or billionaire, like to think of ourselves as fine and good and noble of heart. We all have pride and love and respect for things like life and liberty and kids and friends and country and motherhood and Mom's apple pie. The point is, if you want to be a great real-life leader of character, one of the keys that will do veritable wonders to get you there is:

KEY # 4: AROUSE PRIDE AND THE EMOTIONS

Now I'm not suggesting that you ever risk putting yourself in the dangerous position I was in to do that. But, as I look back, I realize that Willie and Smitty came to my rescue when their pride and emotions were aroused because saving someone's life compassionately touched their natural moral sense and called upon some deep moral motives. So, to <u>AROUSE PRIDE AND THE EMOTIONS</u> in order to get people to want to follow you <u>willingly and voluntarily</u>, think of ways to:

1.) – CALL ON THE NOBLE MOTIVES

I'll bet I know what you're saying to yourself right about now. You're probably saying, "He said a <u>miracle</u> saved him from being murdered. Now he tells me it was noble motives or something like that. What happened to the miracle?"

Well, if that's what you're thinking to yourself, I can say that I'd be thinking about the same thing at this point if I were you. Therefore, I'll be honest with you. Is saying, "a miracle saved me" an accurate statement? To tell you the truth, it isn't. It's actually an understatement. That's right, I said an <u>understatement</u>. How can I say that? Because the story is not yet finished. Here's the rest of the story.

Years had passed since my lurid experience of almost being strangled to death. I was working for the Paterson Post Office as a mailman during one summer when I was still attending Rutgers College of Engineering. My delivery route was in the River Street Section of Paterson. On the day of the month when welfare and unemployment checks come out to be delivered by the mailman, I was kneeling down and making the usual pickup from the en-route box on River Street. All of a sudden, two guys jumped me from behind. They obviously wanted to steal all of this month's money and checks, along with the rest of the mail. One guy got me in a chokehold around the neck using the deadly Japanese stranglehold. The other guy was just beating me up all over with his fists. And I could hardly believe my eyes. The guy punching me was the same guy who had tried to kill me with the chain years ago after the football game.

I could hardly breathe. Just like back then, I was beginning to go unconscious. The thought flashed through my mind, "This is really it, this time. This guy -- the same one as years ago -- is finally going to get me. I must be a victim of fate or something. I'm going to die right out here on a city street in broad daylight."

Just then, two big black guys came running over to my rescue and beat the robbers off. As I was trying to stagger to my feet to thank the two heroes, I looked up and "lo and behold" guess what I saw? There they were. The two guys who had come to my rescue were none other than my old friends Willie and Smitty! I had not seen them for years. What a reunion! They had saved me a second time from being strangled to death. Isn't that eerie?

Now, you may be saying it's just a coincidence. I say it's a little miracle. It had to be a little gift from God because ..... well, consider this: It was enough of a miracle that they had stepped up and saved my life once before back when I was twelve years old. But, the same two guys, Willie and Smitty, just happening to be back in Paterson at the same time after all these years; and just happening to have the same idea to visit someone in that section of Paterson; and just happening to be doing that on the same day; and just happening to be on the same street at the same time; and just happening to be there at the very same time that I was there; and just happening to come upon the vile scene at the moment that the two thugs were trying to rob, and kill me; and just happening to save me in the nick of time from being killed by the same guy who came so close to killing me so many years ago? In short, too many things had to come together at once to be a coincidence. I say it was Providence at work. It was a miracle. I guess maybe God just didn't want me yet!

It shows that people never change. Once again, seeing someone's life in peril, and saving everyone's money, would

CALL ON THE NOBLE MOTIVES in the mind and heart of Willie and Smitty.

From time immemorial, there have been an abundance of powerful illustrations of the sheer wonders that can be achieved when leaders intentionally CALL ON THE NOBLE MOTIVES. For example, the Greek historian Thucydides, in his *History of the Peloponnesian Wars*, tells us that the great Greek statesman, Pericles, did that with his funeral oration for Athenian soldiers who had unwillingly joined their ancestors due to their fighting in the Peloponnesian War's battles between Athens and Sparta. He did so to <u>AROUSE PRIDE AND THE EMOTIONS</u> in the hearts of Athenians on the home front in the hope of shoring up their plummeting morale, and spurring them on to continue to support the war. He would CALL ON THE NOBLE MOTIVES with a historic speech. Here's a part of it:

"It was for this city of ours, then, that these dead warriors of ours so nobly gave their lives in battle elsewhere. Every man who now survives these warriors should gladly continue to toil and fight on behalf of them and our city."

The Funeral Oration by Pericles in 431 BC, of which I have just given you a short snippet, rallied a resurgence of citizen support for the war against Sparta. It inspired the Athenians to continue their toil and keep up their fighting spirit by calling upon noble motives, like not allowing their young men to have died in vain, and by preserving, protecting, and defending loved ones and the Athenian way of life at home in Athens by doing the fighting, bleeding, and dying elsewhere.

Everyone knows about our American Revolutionary War in 1776, and many people have probably heard of the very bloody cataclysmic French Revolution in which hundreds of people were beheaded in public at the guillotine in 1789. But, did you know that Britain, in 1642, also had its own English Revolution long before those? Yes, and a bloody one it was, too. It was when Oliver Cromwell raised an army of poor people and oppressed Puritans, and garnered the support of Parliament, to overthrow the Crown and chop off King Charles I's head and install an English Republic.

What in the world do you think Oliver Cromwell could have done to have given hundreds of thousands of ordinary people the newly found "cojones" to put down their pitchforks, pick up their muskets, and march with him to make such a bloody and incredible feat happen as taking down the powerful English King and Crown? What a challenge! And do you know what his answer was to that question? The answer was: CALL ON THE NOBLE MOTIVES. He exhorted the Puritans to fight for their freedom to worship, and make Puritanism a privileged religion in England. He assured his men that they were following God's law in saving England from the "bloodsuckers" of the King and his Court. And, he prodded the folks to restore the cherished Saxon liberties that every Englishman once had the privilege of enjoying under the Ancient Constitution. That was way back before William the Conqueror came across the English Channel from Normandy and stole them away after defeating the Saxons at Hastings in 1066 AD.

Though England gained a form of Parliamentary Republic, Cromwell had guaranteed himself somewhat dictatorial powers over Parliament by retaining his Revolutionary Army as a standing army whose allegiance continued to be solely to him. He had a fifteen-year stretch of running England before he "changed worlds." With him forever died his republican movement against kings and monarchies. There was no one to replace him, so a king and parliament stepped right back in to rule England.

Cromwell's Revolution was a tutorial for America's founding fathers. It taught them that the English King and Crown tied their shoes one foot at a time like anyone else, and that a few sparks of discontent can become a major firestorm of revolution and independence. The very reason for our existence, as stated by Thomas Jefferson in the Declaration of Independence, is not only based upon ideas of the great philosophers and upon England's great philosopher, John Locke, but actually taken from some of the ideas that Oliver Cromwell had put forth about God and the Ancient Constitution to arouse fellow Englishmen. That's why the "Declaration of Independence" would also CALL ON THE NOBLE MOTIVES of fellow Americans, saying:

"The Laws of Nature and Nature's God entitle America to be separate from, and equal to England; the Creator endowed us with unalienable rights such as Life, Liberty, and the pursuit of Happiness; it is not only our God-given Right, but our Duty, to abolish any Form of Government that is destructive to these ends; that in addition to a firm reliance on divine Providence, the leaders -- the founding fathers -- solemnly pledge their own Lives, Fortunes, and Sacred Honor."

Eight years before the Newburgh Conspiracy, at a time when our American Revolutionary War for Independence was still in its infancy, General George Washington used the Declaration of Independence to CALL ON THE NOBLE MOTIVES as an inspiration to his troops. At six o'clock in the evening on the 9th of July in 1776, Washington gave the order that his copy of the Declaration of Independence be read to all of his men in their individual encampments in and around New York.

It worked like a charm. Although they were bruised and bloodied (as expected) by the devastating power punches of the British Army and Navy at battles in New York, New Jersey, and Pennsylvania, Washington's rag-tag little army was inspirited enough by the noble motives to refuse to stay down for the count. Instead, they continued to boldly and bravely get up again and again, after being knocked down in round after round, so as to stand to fight another day. George Washington had his troops unshakably sticking to the belief that their day would come. As we know, it did.

CALL ON THE NOBLE MOTIVES worked wonders for General Washington back in 1776. But, there may never before in history have been anything as uniquely important to America, or even to the world, as the clash of bona-fide noble motives held by the opposing sides of our American war between the States.

The winning side always gets to write the history. Therefore, the war between the Sates has been named the "American Civil War." Had the Confederate States of America been victorious, it probably would have been named "The Union-Confederate War" or "The Confederate Revolutionary War" for the same reason our war with England was named "The American Revolutionary War".

In 1776, America's founders told England's King George III in the Declaration of Independence that the individual thirteen colonies had the God-given Right, indeed Duty, to remove themselves from being part of any government that is inimical or destructive to their well being. Likewise in 1861, Jefferson Davis and the leaders of eleven Southern States, in seceding from the United States of America, did, for the same reasons, declare their Right to remove themselves. They declared, as in the "Declaration of Independence", that their God given Rights, and the U.S. Constitution's own Tenth Amendment, gave them just cause to remove themselves -- resign from the United States -- and go on to form a brand-new country, like America's founders did.

So, eleven States resigned and formed a separate new nation that they called The Confederate States of America. They used the United States Constitution as the model for their Confederate Constitution, and added a few new wrinkles. The most notable ones outlawed the African slave trade, believe it or not, and added the word "God" throughout the text. They would AROUSE PRIDE AND THE EMOTIONS in the hearts of Southerners by declaring they only wanted to be, and had the right to be, left alone and live in peace as a sovereign nation.

Did you know that President James Buchanan, near the end of his presidential term in 1860, declared he would not oppose the resignation (the secession) of the Southern States from the Union? Incoming President Abraham Lincoln refused to do the same. He vowed that he would kill off any resignations -- by force, if necessary. Thus, a war began.

After the first shots were fired at Fort Sumter in South Carolina, the Lincoln folks flexed their muscles by marching the Federal Army into Virginia to occupy the South. Jefferson Davis, now the duly elected President of the Confederate States of America, condemned it as an invasion of a separate sovereign nation by its neighbor. He would CALL ON THE NOBLE MOTIVES -- self-defense of homeland, property, and family -- to successfully <u>AROUSE PRIDE AND THE EMOTIONS</u>. Like honey attracts bees, that attracted tens of thousands of young men to leave behind home and loved ones and gallop off in glory to join the fight to defend the South's sovereignty and independence. To those eleven Southern States that were now, in fact, a separate nation called the Confederate States of America, President Jefferson Davis' invocations were noble causes, and they hoped that everyone around the world would feel their pain.

Northerners and Europeans did not feel their pain, at all. Why not? It's because wise old Abe Lincoln did young Jeff Davis one better in the clash between the two sides to CALL ON THE NOBLE MOTIVES. Lincoln got his supporters in the North to pitch the fighting as civil strife within a single country, not a war between two sovereign countries. They said the North was only waging a war against some rogue Southern states for the noble cause of abolishing slavery. Although certainly a noble cause, there were many who simply did not buy into slavery as the cause of the war, saying, if that were true, a war would have happened decades ago. Fortunately for Abraham Lincoln, however, a majority <u>did</u> buy into slavery as his reason for waging war on the South.

Lincoln's diplomatic campaign to paint the fighting, brother against brother, in the color of slavery was a superb idea. Most people who counted felt that abolishing slavery was a higher noble cause than the South's dream of, and "Right" to, sovereignty. And Lincoln knew the Europeans had no stomach to be seen as supporting slavery. Consequently, Jefferson Davis failed in his bid to garner the crucial support he needed from Europe.

Abraham Lincoln's decision to CALL ON THE NOBLE MOTIVES as his central leadership theme did, in fact, <u>AROUSE PRIDE AND THE EMOTIONS</u>. To Jeff Davis' horror, it successfully awakened the sleeping giant in the North. Lincoln's great real-life leadership also won over the moral and diplomatic support of the key countries of Europe, whose economic support, as I have said, was desperately needed by the Confederacy to win what became the bloodiest war in history for Americans.

The point of my telling you about this historic display of great real-life leadership within America is to again show you this: to be a great leader of character -- to get people who are under your leadership to <u>want</u> to follow and cooperate <u>willingly and voluntarily</u> -- one of the things you can do is <u>AROUSE PRIDE AND THE EMOTIONS</u>. And, a very, very powerful way to do that is to CALL ON THE NOBLE MOTIVES. It's a call and an appeal that everyone loves, and few wish to turn away, even if they have other motives -- somewhat like a favorite cuddly blanket on a cold winter night that provides "cover" while letting you feel warm and cozy inside.

Here's another appeal everyone loves. As the story goes, Henry Ford, the inventor of the mass-produced automobile, was once visiting his ancestral home in Ireland. When he met with the vicar and elders of the local church, they cried in their Guinness (beer) to him about their financial woes and their crumbling historic structures. The multi-millionaire Ford offered to donate $15,000 to help ease their plight. That was a lot of money in the early 1900's.

The next day, the local newspaper had this headline: "American millionaire donates <u>$50,000</u>." The whole town was buzzing with people in the streets saying to each other, "What a wonderful man is that Henry Ford."

When Ford read the newspaper, he immediately contacted the vicar and church elders. They apologized, saying, "We shall immediately contact the newspaper and ask them to print a retraction saying: 'Correction. American millionaire Ford donates $15,000, not $50,000'. Will that be all right, Mr. Ford?"

Henry Ford thought about it, and thought about his reputation. Then, as the story goes, he went back to them and told them this. "I'll give you the additional $35,000 -- provided that your stone archway at the church, in recognition of my support, has the following words carved on it: 'I came to you, and you took me in. Henry Ford'."

Here's why I told you this story. The church got Henry Ford to cough up an additional $35,000 because they knew how powerful an appeal it is to:

2.) – GIVE PEOPLE A LOFTY REPUTATION TO LIVE UP TO

An appeal that everyone loved, and a display of how to <u>AROUSE PRIDE AND THE EMOTIONS</u> (seventy-five years after the Civil War and almost forty years after Ford's invention) that became more singularly important to the world than almost anything else in history was given to us by Great Britain's prime minister, Winston Churchill, during the Second World War from 1939 to 1945.

They say, if God had not made a Winston Churchill, someone would have had to invent him. When few in the world could foresee a colossal war approaching, Churchill trumpeted the alarm to the free world. He possessed the foresight and the wisdom to recognize what was building over in Germany.

Adolf Hitler's violent religion of Aryan-Fascism was being tolerated by the good people of Germany, one of the most rapidly modernizing countries in Europe. And Hitler's Germany was quickly and quietly forging ahead with the science, engineering, and production of weapons of mass destruction in violation of the Treaty of Versailles and other agreements. To Hitler, Aryan-Fascism and weapons of mass destruction for war were perfect partners. Yes, perfect for Hitler; lethal for civilization.

Churchill understood the Aryan-Fascist religion. Most thoughtless dilettantes and incorrigibly appeasing purblind worldlings of the day did not. Churchill saw that there was little hope left of reconciling with the root objectives and the worldview and the collective derangement of an Aryan-Fascism, which Hitler called Nazism, that was carrying out its goals in a secretive and systematic and scientific, but wholly savage way. Deranged? Savage? …. Definitely! What else would you call harvesting people's bodies to make soap, after murdering them en masse in showers of, not water, but poisonous gas? I can't imagine what the victims' last living thoughts were.

It was in that atmosphere, when the jaws of the devil gaped at Britain, and the evils of Adolf Hitler's Aryan-Fascist religion of terror and torture was spreading throughout Europe, that Churchill hammered away at Hitler, through speeches over the radio, to make the world aware of what was going on, and to AROUSE PRIDE AND THE EMOTIONS within his own "land of hope and glory." During the darkest hours of the war, when Nazi Germany was overrunning all of Europe, and Britain was standing alone against Hitler's relentless onslaught, Churchill would CALL ON THE NOBLE MOTIVES to whip up the British people's spirits. For example, in one of his most inspirational speeches, his response to Hitler's Aryan-Fascist propaganda via the radio into Britain, and threats of an invasion, was:

"We shall defend our island, whatever the cost may be; we shall fight on the beaches, we shall fight on the landing grounds, we shall fight in the fields and in the streets... we shall fight in the hills; but, we shall never surrender."

Churchill went on to say:

"If we fail, the whole world... including all that we have known and cared for, will sink into the abyss of a new Dark Age, made ever more sinister, and perhaps more prolonged, by the lights of (Hitler's) perverted science."

Just as important, continuing to regularly address his fellow Britons by radio, he would never fail to remind them of the historic qualities they may have forgotten they possessed -- Spanish Armada, Trafalgar, Waterloo, Battles of the Somme -- and in doing so, he would automatically GIVE PEOPLE A LOFTY REPUTATION TO LIVE UP TO.

He did an awesome job of bolstering people's spirits. For example, by almost superhuman exertions, thousands of British civilians in their little boats helped rescue over 338,000 British soldiers and Marines who had been trapped with their backs against the sea, like cattle for the slaughter, on the beaches of Dunkirk, France. And, the entire British population stood tall during The Blitz, and Hitler's seventy-one air raids on London, and fifty-six air raids on other cities in England (which in the end, took nearly sixty thousand civilian lives). Churchill continued to embolden his compatriots and encourage them to securely retighten the lug nuts of their defensive armor, by saying:

" If the British Empire should last for a thousand years, men will still look back and say, 'This was their finest hour'."

When Hitler tried to wipe out the Royal Air Force in preparation for an invasion of England, British pilots and engineers, armed with their new Spitfire fighter planes and new secret weapon they had recently invented called "radar", won a decisive victory over the Luftwaffe in the air war over England. Hitler was forced to abandon his invasion of England indefinitely. This "Battle of Britain" once more inspired Churchill to GIVE PEOPLE A LOFTY REPUTATION TO LIVE UP TO in a now famous speech in which he said:

"Never in the field of human conflict was so much owed to so few by so many."

Winston Churchill is considered by many to be the greatest leader of the twentieth century. His dogged, steadfast courage and his great leadership ability to <u>AROUSE PRIDE AND THE EMOTIONS</u> pulled Britain (and the rest of the free democratic world with it) from the jaws of defeat and on to final victory in the most apocalyptic conflict the world has ever seen in which fifty-five million -- that's right -- fifty-five million people were killed, twenty-five million military and thirty million civilians.

The numbers of military and civilians killed during the Second World War might have been even higher if it were not, as some say, for American General George S. Patton. Most objective historians and several books give him credit for having shortened the War. How so? Because he possessed, surprisingly similar to Winston Churchill, dogged, steadfast, aggressive leadership, and thus, he pushed his Third Army across Europe like a wave of bloodhounds relentlessly hunting down a fox, smashing Hitler's armies in its wake.

Patton had another one of Winston Churchill's leadership penchants. He made sure he touched base with his people, which in Patton's case were his troops, regularly and often in order to implement the philosophy GIVE PEOPLE A LOFTY REPUTATION TO LIVE UP TO. For example, near the beginning of the war, he was given command of the American Second Corps after its disastrous defeat at the hands of General Erwin Rommel, the Desert Fox, at the Kasserine Pass in Tunisia, North Africa. As a result of that defeat, British General Alexander (who had overall command) considered American soldiers to be of poor fighting quality. As far as he was concerned, they were all dressed up for the dance, but didn't know how to dance. Patton was given the challenging and unenviable job of finding the problems and restoring the image and self-respect of the American fighting man. He had only eleven days before the next battle in which to galvanize those troops. And galvanize them he did.

He began by shaking his men out of what had become slovenly habits that weaken men's morale, health, and strength. He commandingly enforced military order and discipline. Then he made certain that he kept his part of the bargain by giving them clean clothing, new equipment, hot showers, well-cooked meals, fast mail deliveries, and regular rest. And, he was like a cyclone whirling through his army, seemingly being everywhere at the same time, giving pep talk after pep talk. In the interests of his troops, he reluctantly followed Alexander's orders to the letter, for he always believed, "if you treat a skunk nicely, he will not piss on you -- as often."

As Churchill had reminded the <u>British</u> people, Patton reminded his <u>American</u> people (troops) over and over again of the historic soldiering and fighting qualities of the American fighting man that they may have forgotten they possessed. Thus, the morale of the Second Corps began to soar. Everywhere Patton went, his quality of great real-life leadership electrified and energized his men as he constantly assured them that they would win the next battle. His simple, pride-building exhortations like: "You are Americans, therefore you will utterly defeat the enemy," and "I know you will be worthy" infected his troops with his own strength and self-confidence.

Everything he did, worked. They did defeat the Afrika Corps in the next battle, at El Guettar. And Patton, as usual, heaped praise on his men. He used their success to justify and fertilize his having given them a lofty reputation to live up to by standing before them in full dress, with brass and metals glittering in the African sunshine, and telling them:

"Due to your united efforts and to the manifest assistance of Almighty God, the splendid record of the American Army has attained added luster."

Patton gave the American soldiers in Africa their self-respect back.

Months later, now in command of the Third Army in Europe, he addressed his troops saying:

"I can assure you that the United States Third Army will be the greatest army in American history. The great successes we have achieved together have been due primarily to the fighting heart of America."

And Patton missed no opportunity and spared no effort to see to it that his men's heroics were written-up and published in each man's hometown newspaper.

In December of 1944, like the favorite aunt who never forgets you at Christmas, Patton, as he always did, took the trouble to write a card to each and every man in his Third Army, having his Christmas wish on one side, and a prayer on the other. The card had this inscription of inspiration from Patton to everyone, regardless of religion:

"I have full confidence in your courage, devotion to duty, and skill in battle. We march in our might to complete victory. May God's blessings rest upon each of you on this Christmas Day."

That year, his New Year's message to his men was:

"Your record has been one of continuous victory. Not only have you invariably defeated a cunning and ruthless enemy, the speed and brilliancy of your achievements are unsurpassed in military history."

On New Year's Day of 1945, during a press conference he held to specifically talk about his Third Army's most recent victory, he loudly and publicly proclaimed for the whole world to hear:

"To me, it is a never-ending marvel what our soldiers can do. The people who actually did it were the younger officers and soldiers -- a very marvelous feat. I know of no equal to it in military history. I take my hat off to them."

George S. Patton has been called one of the greatest generals America has ever produced, and the greatest combat leader of modern times. But he was also something else. He was a great real-life leader – period. He infected people with his own burning desire and dogged determination for victory because he would always find a way to GIVE PEOPLE A LOFTY REPUTATION TO LIVE UP TO. He showered his troops with bouquets of sincere praise and approbation, and put them up on a pedestal that they would fight tooth and nail not to be knocked off of.

Before his "last stand," he had been making the rounds among his men (what he always said was the best part of his job) to personally address them for the last time before being redeployed. What he said to his troops takes us forward to our third way to AROUSE PRIDE AND THE EMOTIONS. Again reminding them of the lofty reputation they were carrying forward, "old blood and guts" stepped before them for the last time to:

3.) – THROW DOWN A CHALLENGE

His swansong to them was to cut them loose onto the path of continued victory by challenging them with the simple words: "Show the world how great you are …… where ever you may go."

That was the Patton way of leadership, the thing that set him apart from others. That's what instantly transformed him from a man to a legend, and from a general to a folk hero, when his "last stand" proved to be an untimely death in a suspicious car crash near Mannheim, Germany shortly after Nazi Germany had surrendered. It was untimely in that he never got to do what he had strongly advocated doing: finish the job in Europe by going on to push the newly threatening Communist Russian Armies back to their own borders.

Thousands upon thousands of men, inspired by Patton's challenge, would go on and confidentially show the world how great they, as Americans, were. And, with tears in their eyes when learning of Patton's death, thousands upon thousands would mournfully but proudly reminisce, "I rolled with Patton."

On a cold wintry morning in January of 1961, thousands of people rolled into Washington D.C. and poured onto the lawns and grounds around the Capitol Building. Why were they standing out there for hours and hours in the blustering cold wind? What in the world were they waiting for? Was it an "Elvis" musical concert; or a rally by the ever-growing popular Martin Luther King; or the starting gun of a marathon race? No. Those thousands of men and women were waiting there to see what was actually the end of a different kind of marathon race and the starting gun of a momentous event to be held for the most important of all celebrities. They were there to see the Presidential Inaugural Address of newly elected "Number 35", John Fitzgerald Kennedy,

Sneak previews given to the press promised that Kennedy would <u>AROUSE PRIDE AND THE EMOTIONS</u> with his speech. He did. And, how would he do that? He would THROW DOWN A CHALLENGE. He would proceed to challenge the American people to (in his own words):

"Dare not forget that we are the heirs of that first revolution. …. That the torch has been passed to a new generation of Americans …. unwilling to permit the undoing of those human rights to which this Nation has always been committed ….";

"Pay any price, bear any burden, meet any hardship, support any friend, oppose any foe, in order to assure the survival and success of liberty";

"Ask not what America will do for you, but what together we can do for the freedom of the world";

"Ask not what your country can do for you …. Ask what you can do for your country" (his most famous words).

Those ideas were not new. He had utilized them to THROW DOWN A CHALLENGE to the American electorate during his recent presidential campaign so that he could persuade great masses of people to want to follow him willingly, i.e., want to vote for him. It worked. Tens of millions voted for him!

A few months later, on April 12th, America's Cold War opponent, the USSR, shocked us when they sent up a Russian rocket carrying the first man to travel in space, Yuri Gegarin. The age of man in space had begun.

But the "space race" between the USSR and the USA had actually begun four years earlier. Russian technology had challenged and humiliated the American technological community by launching into space the unmanned satellite, Sputnik I, weighing in the hundreds of pounds. Our answer, our first satellite, which weighed a mere three pounds, ended in disaster when it caught fire during the lift-off stage. A sad little beeping sound from the satellite at the launch site was all that could be heard as it fizzled-out.

For the next several years our government, as a consequence, threw down a challenge of its own. They called on youngsters who could handle math and science to study engineering and the sciences in college to help our country engage and beat the USSR in the "space race". Many thousands of young people, who probably otherwise would not have done so, took up that challenge. How do I know? I remember. I was there. And I was one of them.

Shortly after his inauguration, Kennedy proceeded in May of 1961 to again THROW DOWN A CHALLENGE. He called upon our Space Agency, our American technological community, and the U.S. Congress to cooperate in achieving a phenomenal goal: Be the first to land a man on the moon and return him safely to Earth -- and do it before the end of the decade. His leadership succeeded in achieving the first step -- the cooperation of Congress -- for, soon after he threw down that challenge, the money was approved for attempting to put a man on the moon, the most expensive non-military venture in the history of Earth.

John F. Kennedy would not live to see his fellow Americans successfully land on the moon. His "last stand" would be that shocking assassination by a certifiable nutcase, Lee Harvey

Oswald, on November 22, 1963. But his great leadership would ultimately pay off. Six years later, Neil Armstrong (a Purdue graduate) who was the mission commander and first one down, and Buzz Aldrin (a West Point graduate), became the first human beings to step foot on the moon and go for a walk on its surface. It was June 20, 1969. John F. Kennedy's challenge had been met, and with six months to spare!

I'm going to tell you about another kind of "last stand", by another West Point graduate. No, I don't mean George Armstrong Custer, as in "Custer's Last Stand". I mean the man who many think was America's greatest twentieth century five-star general -- Douglas MacArthur.

Volumes have been written about MacArthur, such as William Manchester's book *American Caesar: Douglas MacArthur*. The "American Caesar's" story is so fascinating, it is almost mystically pulling me to tell you about it right here and now. However, I could not possibly do justice to such an awesome story, and shouldn't try to, in a book like this whose purpose is to show you how to be a great real-life leader. But I see no reason why I shouldn't pass on to you the benefit of one small, but awe-inspiring piece of his story which is a marvelous example of all three ways to implement our KEY # 4 : AROUSE PRIDE AND THE EMOTIONS. I want to tell you about his farewell speech on May 12, 1962 to his beloved West Point. It turned out to be a farewell speech -- his last stand -- to his beloved American people.

During that speech, he would CALL ON THE NOBLE MOTIVES, and that applied to all, yes all, future leaders of America (not just cadets). Here is a composite of his words and ideas:

"Be strong enough to know when you are weak, and brave enough to face yourself when you are afraid;

Be proud and unbending in honest failure, but humble and gentle in success;

Do not substitute words for actions nor seek the path of comfort, but face the stress and spur of difficulty and challenge;

Learn to stand up in the storm, but have compassion for those who fall;

Learn to laugh, yet never forget how to weep;

Reach into the future, yet never neglect the past;

Be serious, yet never take yourself too seriously;

<u>Master yourself, before you seek to master others</u>."

He then went on in his address to GIVE PEOPLE A LOFTY REPUTATION TO LIVE UP TO by reminding the Corps of Cadets that they are following close order behind West Point's sons of an earlier day to be America's lifeguards and gladiators and war-guardians in the arena of battle and in the raging tides of international conflict. He said:

"The Long Gray Line of West Point sons, The Corps, has never failed America. If it were to do so, a million ghosts in olive drab, in brown khaki, in blue and gray, would rise from their white crosses thundering those magic words -- Duty, Honor, Country. .... You are the leaven which binds together America's defense. .... You are the great leaders who will determine America's destiny the moment the war tocsin sounds."

He continued his speech with warning them not to be war mongers, but to be leaders who above all other leaders pray for peace, resurrecting what Plato said:

"For you must suffer and bear the deepest scars and wounds of war .... and only the dead have seen the end of war."

During a previous joint session of Congress in his honor, he drew tears and removed old wounds, with the care and skill of a surgeon, in a speech that ended with his famous words, "old soldiers never die, they just fade away." Now, in his final address to West Point, he went on to THROW DOWN A CHALLENGE to those in the Corps sitting before him in West

Point's magnificent Washington Hall (actually the "mess hall") to take up the mantle that he now had to pass on, as he poignantly spoke these final words:

"The shadows are lengthening for me. The twilight is here. My days of old have vanished. Watered by the tears .... caressed by the smiles of yesterday, I listen vainly for the witching melody of faint bugles blowing reveille; of far drums beating the long roll. In my dreams I hear again .... the mournful mutter of the battlefield. But in the evening of my memory, always I come back to West Point. .... Today marks my final roll call with you, but I want you to know that, when I cross the river, my last conscious thoughts will be of the Corps, and the Corps, and the Corps. ------- I bid you farewell."

When he finished, there was a moment of breathtaking silence. Not only the words he spoke, but his quiet, sincere tone, and the mellowed texture of an old soldier's voice touched everyone. Most eyes were glazed over. Many were filled with tears.

America was losing its last great military genius. Was that a turning point in American military history? There was already an enormously foreboding sense of occasion there that day, as if everyone had just lost a beloved old grandfather. And how do I know that, not having been there? It was told to me by Brigadier General Carl Morin and others who were there that day, and who themselves have now become those West Point sons of an earlier day -- those gladiators in the raging tides of international conflict -- who led American soldiers in a war on the other side of the world in Vietnam that halted the "domino effect" of the USSR's dream of world communism. That war helped to lay the foundation for our ultimate victory in the Cold War and for the demise of the despised Berlin Wall.

General Douglas MacArthur would "cross the river" less than two years after his address at West Point.

Another two decades went by before an admirer of General Douglas MacArthur would finish building on the foundation laid down by MacArthur and those future leaders he addressed while at West Point that day. This was a special admirer. He would be the one who would finally win the Cold War against the Communist USSR and live to see that despised Berlin Wall crash down. That admirer would be none other than our President Ronald Reagan again.

By 1987, Reagan had the USSR pretty much on the run, despite the Soviet Politburo's selection of a young, clever, vigorous Mikhail Gorbachev as their new General Secretary. Here's how he did it

There had been two schools of thought in the USSR on how to bring the whole world under the heel of the USSR's communist philosophy and domination, which both schools agreed had to happen for communism to work. The first school wanted it done right away. It said, if they wipe out the USA (their single biggest obstacle) with nuclear weapons, the rest of the world will easily fall into line. The second, more patient school believed that the capitalist USA would collapse on its own , economically, as Karl Marx had calculated it would. But now, with Mikhail Gorbachev, was there possibly a third way that was acceptable to the Soviets?

The USSR and the USA were loosely following a relationship of "glasnost" and '"perestroika" -- openness and peaceful coexistence. Could that continue, along with a Cold War policy that allowed other nations to freely, not forcibly, choose to join one camp or the other based on what they wanted to do?

Gorbachev had little choice, for here's what Reagan had done to put the USSR's first and second schools of thought "behind the eight-ball." His buildup of America's military forces, coupled with MAD (mutually assured destruction) and his new Strategic Defense Initiative (SDI) that could shoot down nuclear missiles before they reach the USA (flippantly called "Star Wars" by many in the press) reduced the USSR's first school of thought to somewhat of a doomsday scenario, for them. For, prior to the "nuclear umbrella" created by Reagan's Strategic Defense Initiative, an analysis by the Pentagon (and you can bet by the Kremlin, too) had said that over 150 million people would die in a nuclear exchange between the USSR and the USA -- on the side that "won", if the MAD standoff failed. And what would happen if rogue nations became nuclear, or if another Hitler came along? It's what Reagan came to refer to as the nightmare of "Nuts and Nukes". Reagan said (and Gorbachev probably concurred):

"That's not the kind of thing that makes you sleep better at night."

But now the USA would have a nuclear umbrella. The USSR would not.

As for the USSR's second school of thought based on Karl Marx's calculations, just the opposite was happening. Reagan had the American economy booming. Far from the economic collapse that was predicted by Karl Marx, it was better than ever. On the other hand, the USSR's socialist economy was the one that was tanking and crumbling and collapsing. No way could the USSR keep up with the American economic juggernaut. And Mikhail Gorbachev knew it.

With the Communist USSR's two traditional schools of thought now gravely weakened by Reagan, Gorbachev had gotten to blatantly coveting the allegiances of other nations and selling the USSR as the good guys. Reagan had previously labeled the USSR as "the evil empire" because of the Gulags with their despicable human conditions, because of the Berlin wall, because of the lack of rights and freedoms of press, speech, religion, and everything else that US citizens enjoyed. Despite all of those obvious violations against humanity, Gorbachev still claimed that the USSR had freedom, and openness, and prosperity, and human liberties just as good, if not better, than in the USA. Can you believe the man's b---s?

Although Reagan and Gorbachev had come to rub along together in a historic relationship of respect and friendliness and understanding and good communications, Reagan, like the betrayed party in a divorce case, wanted to remedy Gorbachev's trying to make a fool of him by cleverly trying to make the world think the USSR already had the freedoms he was perhaps personally leaning toward, but in fact, <u>did not</u> have. So Reagan jumped on the opportunity to turn the tables on Gorbachev and call him out on freedom. Because Gorbachev was mouthing off, and actually leaning in the direction of greater freedoms for the USSR and the Eastern Bloc, Reagan decided to THROW DOWN A CHALLENGE that would "help Gorbachev along" with a little extra push in that direction. He would, essentially, say to the world, "Okay, if Gorbachev and the Soviets really do have freedom and glasnost and perestroika, then 'res ipsa loquitur', let the situation speak for itself." He arranged a trip to West Berlin, and, while standing just a few yards from the hated Berlin Wall and looking toward it, he leveled this now famous and historic challenge:

"This is one sign the Soviets can make that would be unmistakable -- and that would advance dramatically the cause of freedom and peace."
"General Secretary Gorbachev, if you seek peace, if you seek prosperity for the Soviet Union and Eastern Europe, if you seek liberalization, come here to this gate. Mr. Gorbachev, open this gate. Mr. Gorbachev, TEAR DOWN THIS WALL!"

Only Heaven knows what went through Mikhail Gorbachev's mind when "Reagan the Lionhearted" gave his dauntless "Tear Down This Wall" speech to boldly THROW DOWN A CHALLENGE to him.
And so, the Berlin Wall came down. And the Communist USSR unraveled. And the entire Communist Eastern European Bloc was dismantled. And, yes, that means we had won the Cold War.

Some skeptics might say, "What you're telling me may be all well and good for Patton and Kennedy and Reagan, but I'd like to know how you can make all of this philosophy work for me."
Well, to start with, it's not just philosophy. Think about it. Haven't we been seeing, all our lives, how the noble motives, and

giving people a lofty reputation to live up to, and throwing down a challenge have worked in practical ways to <u>AROUSE PRIDE AND THE EMOTIONS</u> within people to get them to do things, or not doing things? Don't churches, hospitals, and volunteer groups everywhere CALL ON THE NOBLE MOTIVES to get people to donate their time and money to help with their poor, the sick, the elderly, and their youth? I personally have coached kids, voluntarily, from the Little League level to the high school level in baseball and football for more than a dozen years for that reason. And how about the thousands of those brave and noble kids who grow up, volunteer to join the military, and willingly go off to places like Iraq or Afghanistan? They're examples of the noble motive of protecting their families and loved ones back home by being the "magnets" that attract and fight the terrorists over there, so that we won't have to fight them over here. And how about simply listening to the words of every high school and college alma mater and football "fighting song." Isn't every single one of them based on the practical idea, GIVE PEOPLE A LOFTY REPUTATION TO LIVE UP TO?

I remember an incident involving my friend and football teammate, Richard Ruocco. He was a guard on our team, and had done something wrong during one of our games, as all of us do in football games. But, our coach knew that Ruocco's parents were sitting behind our benches up in the seats of the stadium. So what did the coach do? He used that fact to fire up Ruocco to get him to make bigger and better plays, employing THROW DOWN A CHALLENGE, by saying to him while pointing up to the stands, "Your mother and father are up there watching you; think of <u>them</u>; they probably hear people around them talking about you; think of your reputation and good name; make your mother and father proud of you."

I heard our coach, first-hand. I was standing right next to him. And I saw what happened in the second half. Ruocco made his mother and father proud of him!

When you were a kid, how many times did you have to THROW DOWN A CHALLENGE, or did you hear someone else do so, by saying, "If you do that again (or, don't stop doing that, or, etc.), I'm gonna punch you in the nose"? That scene takes place thousands of times every day.

Speaking of THROW DOWN A CHALLENGE, when I was twelve years old -- playing football with the kids from the Village and the Projects, I used to go to the Central High School football games at Hincliffe Stadium in Paterson, New Jersey and dream of the day when I would be out on that field in front of thousands of football fans. But, my oldest brother Tom (fka, Tony) had, years before, dislocated his collarbone playing for Central. Therefore, Mom and Dad had signed the permission slip for my older brother, Conrad, to play only baseball and basketball, not football. The same was in store for me. Although I still had a year to go before I would be going to Central High School, my Mother had already lowered the boom on me, saying, "Don't you get any ideas about playing football next year, Norman."

During the coming months, I alternately moaned, and begged, and pleaded, and even cried over it. But Mom and Dad stuck to their guns saying, "Your brother got hurt because he was too thin to play football; and so are you". And they told me, "It's your own fault that you're too thin; you never eat all of your supper; you're too picky."

It's true. They had been goading me for years (without success) to get me to eat creamed corn, and this or that kind of vegetable, and a lot of other stuff that is "good for you" that I hated. I still begged and cried a little, and kind of carried on saying, "Awe come on, Ma, all my friends' parents are gonna let them play."

Mom and Dad must have been talking it over and must have decided they would THROW DOWN A CHALLENGE. One day, when I had been begging, Dad said to me, "Okay, if you eat everything we give you, and if you weigh 150 pounds when you're a freshman in high school, we'll sign for you to play football." Boy, was I thrilled.

Wow! What a challenge that was! I was only about 110 pounds! Could I possibly gain 40 pounds in one year? I would have to. For I knew that Dad was secretly on my side, and that's the only way he was able to get Mom to agree to let me play.

I ate so much food during that next year, I think I must have almost "eaten our family out of house and home." I ate everything. One day, I even ate so much creamed corn that I vomited it all back up. Dad periodically weighed me on the bathroom scale. I was steadily becoming "fattened up." Mom and dad were amazed.

When I finally entered high school, Dad took my final weight. I made it. I tipped the scale at 151 pounds. Mom and Dad, true to their promise, signed for me to play football. I was one husky and happy freshman team quarterback. I did soon grow and thin-out, however.

There you have some down-to-earth examples showing that you can AROUSE PRIDE AND THE EMOTIONS to get things done without resorting to complex philosophy or threats or force.

I feel that I would be remiss if I did not tell you the following bizarre, but true, story that I think you will enjoy, which illustrates all three ways I have given you to AROUSE PRIDE AND THE EMOTIONS. It was told to me by Dr. Ernest Gamble, Ph.D., a member of our family. It happened when he was a young tank officer in Europe during World War II. Here it is.

None other than General George S. Patton had made everyone under his command aware that, in past wars, more soldiers had died at the hands of disease and infection due to slovenly hygiene and sanitation than at the hands of the enemy. Patton liked to use that platform to get his army to maintain hygiene and sanitation. How? He would AROUSE PRIDE AND THE EMOTIONS by getting his troops to be their brother's keeper, not only in battle, but also in camp, by telling them they owed it to each other's families and loved ones back home to take care that no one would die from disease or sickness in camp (CALL ON THE NOBLE MOTIVES). He told them he was proud that they had the reputation of being the most sanitary outfit over there in Europe right now (GIVE PEOPLE A LOFTY REPUTATION TO LIVE UP TO). And he promised them certain special privileges because of that reputation -- if they could keep it -- reminding them that a round of inspections by the Inspector General was coming up (THROW DOWN A CHALLENGE).

One day, when the Inspector General was at a regiment commanded by a particularly ambitious officer under Patton, he noticed that everyone in the mess hall had a fork in the upper left-hand pocket of his shirt. The General asked a soldier from the regiment who was assigned to him as a guide, "Why the fork?"

The soldier replied, "In order to maintain sanitary habits, Sir, we never touch any of the food with our hands. If you want a piece of bread, for instance, you or someone else sticks his fork into it and takes it, or passes it on."

The General voiced his approval, saying to the officers with him, "Maybe we ought to use that there forking idea in all of our regiments."

Later, while walking outside, the General noticed that everyone had a white string hanging down from the fly of his pants. He turned to his guide again and asked, "Why the string?"

The soldier once again immediately replied, "In order to maintain sanitary habits, Sir, the string allows one to pull the penis out of the pants to urinate without touching it with the hands."

The General once again approved. He turned to the other officers and said, "Maybe we ought to try that, as well, with all of our troops". Then something occurred to him. He turned to the guide and said, "The string is a good idea, soldier .... but how do you get the penis back inside the pants without touching it?"

With that, the guide stirred and hesitated. Then he replied, "Well, Sir, I don't know about the others ..... but, as for me .... I use the fork!"

The moral of the story is, you can get the most unexpected and spectacular results when you AROUSE PRIDE AND THE EMOTIONS.

Churchill and Patton and Kennedy and Reagan all knew the enormous power that pride and the emotions can wield. Patton's giving troops a lofty reputation to live up to may have shortened the War. Kennedy's and Reagan's throwing down a challenge helped to put men on the Moon and bring down the Berlin Wall, respectively. Even little ole me saw the power that pride and the emotions can wield. My life was saved -- twice -- because of noble motives!

That, dear readers, is the power of pride and the emotions. They are ingredients that every successful person has. They are what makes everything from winning an election, or getting a high paying job, or winning a football game, right down to winning something as simple as a pie eating contest or log rolling competition so important to people.

Since pride and the emotions are such volatile characteristics in the psychology of human relations and great real-life leadership, isn't it the better part of wisdom to try to get people's pride and emotions working <u>for</u> you, rather than <u>against</u> you? How do you do that? You show them that what you want them to do is something that they already believe and already want to do. Once you do that, they will, so to speak, lower the drawbridge, raise the gates, open the doors, and let you into the private fortress of their thoughts and beliefs, and readily accept you as their leader.

So, to become a great real-life leader -- to get people to <u>want</u> to follow you <u>willingly and voluntarily</u> -- a fine and noble and effective way to do that is to use:

<u>KEY # 4: AROUSE PRIDE AND THE EMOTIONS</u>

And, you now have seen examples of how you can do that by using the following techniques:

116

1.) - CALL ON THE NOBLE MOTIVES.

2.) - GIVE PEOPLE A LOFTY REPUTATION TO LIVE UP TO.

3.) – THROW DOWN A CHALLENGE.

Chapter 6: Do This ... And The Whole World Is With You

At 14 years old, young Tom was as close to a Dad as a boy could be. Not only had he been there with his big, hearty, self-made father when he successfully carved a farm out of the wilderness and built a modest house amongst the Indians, but his loving father had taught him how to catch fish, and hunt deer, and ride a horse, and paddle a canoe, and shoot wild turkeys. Although his Dad had no formal schooling himself, he always talked to his son about learning the ABCs, and reading, and writing, and arithmetic. He did the best he could to at least teach his boy how to write his name and say his prayers and read the *Bible*. Dad had constructed an edifice of love and happiness for his son.

Very suddenly one day, without warning, Tom's idyllic edifice came crashing down around him as if it were an actual edifice of stone and wood falling on his head. His inspiration and role model and best friend, his loving Dad, very quickly and shockingly and catastrophically died. Fourteen years old Tom would sooner be struck by lightning. He was shattered.

At the same time he, essentially, lost his mother and became an orphan. For, she too was thunderstruck by her husband's sudden death. And, already crumbling under the emotional stress of caring for Tom's six sisters and his infant brother, this was the straw that broke the camel's back as far as her mental health was concerned. She simply collapsed.

Tom was put under the supervision of guardians. They sent him off to a boarding school whose teacher was a strict clergyman, the "Reverend Mr. Maury." Haunted by the fear of being called a little orphan boy by some of the rascals in that school, and not wanting them to poke fun at the high pitch of his voice, he found it useful to hang out with some bad company. He later said, "When I recollect that my care and direction was thrown upon myself entirely, without relative or friend to advise or guide me, and recollect the various sorts of bad company with which I associated, I am astonished that I did not become as worthless to society as they."

What happened to Tom that stopped him from following bad company off the straight and narrow path? What happened was …. Mr. Maury exercised leadership. He began to help Tom. He began to teach him how to handle the problems and worries and anxieties that were caused by the memory of his father, and by the enduring bond that existed between him, as a 14-year-old boy, and a beloved and idolized, but deceased father. Reverend Maury gave him writings and literature from history about people who, like Tom, had to handle the death of a loved one. He inspired Tom to start a diary of his favorite passages from those writings on which he could lean for emotional support and encouragement. And he pushed the boy to work hard and make sure he kept busy at all times.

That zealous and exacting teacher changed young Tom's life. If it had not been for Mr. Maury's great real-life leadership, young Tom might have grown up to be as worthless to society as some of the wrong kind with whom he had been hanging out. Instead, he grew up to be one of our most respected and important Americans. He went on to write one of the most cherished pieces of work in American history that, today, would fetch hundreds of millions of dollars if it were put on the auction block. You might have heard of our Tom. His full name was Thomas Jefferson. The priceless work he wrote in 1776 was, of course, the "Declaration of Independence."

The point of this true story is: the Reverend Mr. Maury was able to get his pupil, the young Thomas Jefferson, to follow <u>him</u>, rather than follow bad company, by <u>helping</u> him. And he did that by teaching him how to handle the problem of his father's death, and the emotional worry and anxiety that came with it. And that is our:

KEY # 5: HELP PEOPLE

If you help people and teach them, they will like you and need you. If they like you and need you, they will follow you. It's only natural. And it's only natural that when someone needs your help, that means, by definition, they need your help with a problem. So, we're talking about problems here.

Do you know what is the second biggest challenge with any problem? It is solving the problem. Now, you probably would say to me, "What the heck do you mean, second biggest challenge? Solving the problem has to be the first biggest challenge." And to that I would answer, "You would think so. But in the long run, the first biggest challenge with a problem for most people is emotionally handling the problem. Emotional worry and anxiety over a problem can have more serious consequences to your life than the problem itself."

Therefore, when we talk about KEY # 5: HELP PEOPLE, we are talking about helping with a problem. And from there, we are talking about: first, teaching people how to emotionally handle the problem -- how to handle the heavy baggage called worry and anxiety that comes with a problem; second, teaching people the techniques you can use to solve the problem itself.

No one should ever take worry and anxiety over a problem lightly. Those twin "cancers" can bring down the most stoic people. For example, General Ulysses S. Grant, though outwardly appearing unflappable, had difficulty handling worry and anxiety throughout the Civil War. It literally drove him to drink. It almost cost him his command; for example, when his prescription for rest and relaxation to handle the worry and anxiety over past and future battles contained whiskey as a major ingredient. President Lincoln silenced Grant's critics by saying he would send a case of whiskey to every general in the field if that would bring him the victories that Grant was giving him.

By April 8, 1865, in the fifth year of the Civil War, Grant's Union Armies were at last in hot pursuit of General Lee's much smaller, ragged, starving, and exhausted Confederate Army, after having chased it all around Virginia for months. But going head-to-head with Robert E. Lee was always a big headache, and it gave Grant a giant one. Here's what Grant said in his own words in *Personal Memoirs*:

"I was suffering very severely with a sick headache, and stopped at a farmhouse on the road ...... hoping to be cured by morning. I proceeded at an early hour in the morning, still suffering with the headache. When an officer (bearing a message from Lee regarding his surrender) reached me, I was still suffering with the sick headache; but, the instant I saw the contents of the note, I was cured."

The point is: it was worry and anxiety that caused Grant's severe headache and illness. He was not handling worry and anxiety very effectively. But he was cured the instant his mental and emotional outlook changed.

Here's what else worry and anxiety can do to people. You've probably heard the old saw: "You get ulcers from what's eating you, not from what you are eating." Well, it's more than an old saw. The medical profession says that half the people in hospital beds are there for illnesses whose root causes are worry and anxiety. Did you know that worry and anxiety can even cause heart trouble, arthritis, and diabetes? They can make your hair turn gray, even make you lose your hair and go bald. They bring about pimples and skin rashes, and cause wrinkles and lines in your face that can change your expression and ruin your good looks. A dentist in New Jersey, Dr. Ronald Rosen, once told me that worry and anxiety can even cause cavities and discoloration of your teeth by altering your body's calcium balance. Worry and anxiety are also the major causes of suicide in our country. And remember these words: "Funerals and hospital beds come at an expensive price -- and come suddenly -- in this day and age!"

When General George S. Patton was being relentlessly badgered and chastened for slapping, with his gloves, a soldier who was in the hospital for no other reason but worry and anxiety, he said he was just trying to "make him mad and put some fight in him." For Patton, who loved his soldiers and regularly spent time with them, knew more than anyone that every soldier was suffering from worry and anxiety to a greater or lesser degree. He said that if they all gave in to those twin cancers and didn't try to fight them off and handle them everyone would be in the hospital. There would be no army left.

Patton was trying to cut through the blur of psychology by helping men handle worry and anxiety right there on the spot. He reasoned that if the men had already "let their fear overcome their sense of duty," then he had to make them fear him more than the enemy.

Patton's critics did not, but Patton certainly did, know the problem with worry and anxiety that soldiers felt, for he had always made it his policy to visit with, and talk with, hundreds upon hundreds of his troops. And even so celebrated and illustrious a figure as he, like General Grant in the Civil War, had to constantly strive to fight off and handle the problem within himself. Yes, Patton certainly knew the worry and anxiety problem when he saw it. He had it, too!

For example, from North Africa he wrote to his wife (Beatrice), before the attack on Rommel's forces, that he had "as always before an attack, a shortness of breath." And when he visited with his combat troops in forward areas and came under fire once again as he had as a young officer, he secretly confessed to Beatrice:

"I still get scared. I guess I will never get used to it. …. I hate shells and bombs and strafing planes. …. And the profusion of mines laid by the Axis was a distinct mental hazard. …. And when exposed, I felt depressed for about half an hour, and the palms of my hands became moist."

In 1943, on the shelf over the slapping incident, and waiting for his big boss, Chief of Staff George C. Marshall, to get him back into the fight with a new command, he wrote to Beatrice saying:

"This worry and inactivity has raised hell with my insides; but, destiny will keep floating me down the stream of fate; meanwhile, send me some more pink medicine (Pepto Bismol)."

Before the Battle of the Bulge in 1944, Patton wrote to Bea:

"You had better send me a couple of bottles of pink medicine. When I am attacking, I get bilious. I had a bad case of short breath this morning -- my usual reaction to an impending fight or match. I am having indigestion and the heaves as I always do before a match. It is not fear as to the result, but simply the anxiety to get started."

So, one of the most wonderful things you can do as a leader, and in so doing, get people to need you and want to follow you willingly, is implement our <u>KEY # 5: HELP PEOPLE</u> by teaching them how to handle the worry and anxiety associated with a problem. And the first and simplest way you can do that is to help them by teaching them and convincing them how important it is to do as simple a thing as:

1.) – KEEP BUSY

The Reverend Mr. Maury got young Thomas Jefferson to follow him rather than follow the wrong kind of company by keeping him busy with reading about ways to handle his father's death. Thomas Jefferson learned a lifetime lesson from that. Years later when his beloved wife, Martha Wayles Jefferson, died after only ten years of "unchequered" happy marriage together, the only thing that finally brought him back from the brink of disaster, after months and months on the edge due to worry and anxiety and depression caused by his grief, was to KEEP BUSY. He took his seat in Congress at Annapolis and smothered his worry and anxiety by immersing himself in the business of America. And, after each of four of his children and other family and friends died, he conscripted the same remedy: KEEP BUSY.

Perhaps you are asking, "How does keeping busy help people to deal with handling the emotional worry and anxiety that comes with a problem?" The answer is actually simple. Human nature has a way of not allowing you to think about two things at the same time. Did you know that?

Let's do something. Have you ever tried to think about two things at the same time? Check it out for yourself. First close your eyes. Now try to think about what you did at work today at the same time as you try to think about what to have for dinner tonight. Are you ready? Okay. Here we go. .... It's impossible to focus on both at the same time, isn't it! You are able to focus on one, then quickly jump back to the other, but not focus on both exactly at the same time. That's why, when people KEEP BUSY by getting right into working on solving a problem that <u>can</u> be solved, or, KEEP BUSY by getting immersed in some other activity besides thinking about a problem that <u>cannot</u> be solved (such as a death), they are able to handle worry and anxiety. They are able to lose themselves in their work.

Here's how my wife and I did that. On September 11, 2001, a day, like the day Pearl Harbor was attacked, that will live in infamy, Islamic-Fascist terrorists hijacked commercial airplanes and crashed them, kamikazi style, into the Twin Towers skyscrapers in New York City, into the Pentagon in Washington, DC, and were headed for the White House or Capitol Building in Washington, DC.

As everyone knows, both of the Twin Towers collapsed right down to the ground. The Pentagon was badly damaged. The attempted attack on the White House or Capitol was foiled only because of the bravery of airline passengers who caused their plane to crash into a field in Pennsylvania before it could accomplish its ignominious mission. The enemies, who killed 3,000 people that day (more than killed at Pearl Harbor), were not a nation; they were Islamic-Fascist terrorists whose training camps, though in several countries, were headquartered in Afghanistan.

A few weeks later, the first couple of hundred operatives from secret American special operations units were "over there" on one of the most secret and dangerous missions in their history. With that, my wife Diane and I were hit with one of those problems of worry and anxiety that <u>cannot</u> be solved. You see, our son was one of those special operations people "over there."

We could very well have destroyed our health over the worry and anxiety for our son being over there. Where exactly was he? What was he doing? At that very moment, as we spoke, was he safe, or was he fighting for his life? Would he be wounded? Worse? There were no e-mails or telephone calls or even snail-mails allowed. Not knowing what was happening was a killer.

People would ask me, "How can you sleep at night?" I would reply:

"I can't. I'm awake half the night. Now, my wife and I have decided to not just sit glued to the television, constantly looking for little signs of our son and his black helicopter buddies on the news. We decided to crank up our private investment activities so that we are overwhelmed with work. And that has done it. In the whirlwind of our activities throughout the day, there is hardly a minute between what we are doing from moment to moment to think about anything else, as you cannot think about two things at exactly the same time. Now when I finish eating dinner at night, I fall asleep in the easy chair in front of the television, finally watching the news."

We discovered that the best and cheapest medical antidote on the market for handling the natural worry and anxiety that accompanies a problem is: KEEP BUSY.

While we were mentally immersed in our whirlwind of investment activities to KEEP BUSY all day long, we did a second thing to handle the worry and anxiety over our son being under fire in Afghanistan. And it is the second way that you, as a leader, can <u>HELP PEOPLE</u> with a problem. Help them and teach them to:

2.) TAKE ONE DAY AT A TIME

Now I'm certainly not suggesting that you tell people to neglect planning for the future, or remembering the past. Planning must be done, and remembering can be valuable and pleasant. But tell them that, once they've done those things, avoid dwelling on them. Avoid being preoccupied with the past, or worrying about the past. They cannot relive the past. It's gone forever. It will never return. And it can never be altered.

As for the future, who the heck knows? Did you know that, completely beyond our control, we are actually flying through time and space into the future at a speed of nineteen miles per second? Just think about that; Nineteen miles a <u>second</u>. Incredible! Because it's so absolutely beyond our control, how can we possibly know "what the devil" the future toward which we are speeding will be?

It is simply impossible to live in either the future or the past, much less in both at the same time, for even one split second. So, tell your people to not allow their minds to even try to do that. It is only possible to live today -- in the present. Today is the only time over which they can exercise even a modicum of control. Whatever are their problems, or burdens, or challenges, or struggles, or worries, or anxieties, tell them to remember this: It is within their power to handle them for at least this one day -- from morning to bedtime. So, if people you are leading have a problem, help them to TAKE ONE DAY AT A TIME.

I have always admired people who have a gift for putting an important truth in a new and picturesque way. One such person I know is Brigadier General (Ret.) Carl Morin who, as a young high school football star in southern Florida, was recruited by a number of big universities, but ultimately decided on West Point in order to play Army football in the traditions of Glenn Davis and Doc Blanchard, renowned Heisman Trophy winners.

He said his first day at West Point was a shock. Here's how he described it to me:

"We were hustled and hassled and harassed and hurried and humiliated from morning until night with little rest, in typical West Point tradition. It was the longest day of my life. One of the guys grabbed an apple from lunch and carried it around all day, waiting for a spare minute to eat it. That spare minute never came. Finally in our bunks at night, after taps and lights out, I heard him crunch one bite into the apple. Then I heard it drop on the floor. He had taken one bite out of the apple and was so tired that he fell asleep. Meanwhile, I just lay there in my bunk, looking up at the ceiling, saying to myself, 'Oh Mr. Ceiling up there, what have I gotten myself into here? I don't think I want to see you again this time tomorrow night.' But I also said to myself, 'I'm here now, and I've come a long way from Florida to get here; so I'll try one more day.' I did the same thing the next day. And, day after day, I said the same thing."

Cadet Carl Morin managed to take one day at a time. Thirty-one years later he retired as Brigadier General Carl Morin, under offer of promotion to Major General and Deputy Commander of Fort Lewis (which is in the state of Washington).

"Mary Kelly" stopped by my table one day at the West Point Visitor Center when I was doing a book signing for my book *Understanding West Point ... and Thomas Jefferson*. I am calling her by that name, though it is not her real name. I agreed not to reveal her true identity because she told me it would be embarrassing to her and her family if people saw it in print. But "Mary Kelly" is a real person. I can personally vouch for the truth of her story. She stood in front of my table, and, during the lull time of my book-signing day, she poured her heart out to me.

She first approached my table saying, "I originally thought about mailing this letter to you, but since I'm visiting West Point, and you are here, I want to hand it to you in person and tell you how much your book has helped me." I thanked her for those kind words and asked her, like I ask everyone, "How has my book helped you?" That's when she gave me the letter, and told me this story:

"Not long after my son was deployed to Iraq, they came and told me that he was a casualty of the war. My son was dead!

"I was absolutely paralyzed with grief. My boy was all that is fine and patriotic in America -- and young. His teachers always told me that he was one of the exceptional young men of his generation. So why did God allow this to happen to him?

"It seemed like the whole world was crashing down on me. I didn't want to go to work. I didn't want to talk to the rest of my family. I wanted nothing to do with church and God anymore. I was bitter and hostile. Why did my good boy who had his whole life ahead of him have to be killed? I couldn't bear it. I didn't want to live. I planned on taking my own life so I could be with my son. I didn't want him to be alone. He was now alone.

"At the last minute, looking through my drawers for some personal token to hold in my hand while taking my life, I came upon this envelope from my son labeled, 'To be opened only upon my death.' It was, 'To Mom.'

"An angel must have taken my hand and led me to that envelope. Here's what my son wrote in the letter inside of the envelope:

'Dear Mom, Thank you for all the great times we had during my life. Although I'm sad to leave you and all the good times behind, I'm confident my decision to protect you and everyone else was correct. There are many things today we didn't get to say. But thank you for the things in the past you did say that helped me and taught me. Whenever I had a hard time, you always told me to carry on and take it one day at a time. I could not have gotten through the hardships without doing that. So don't be sad. Life must go on. That's why I'm a soldier: to let life go on. If I could come back for just a little while, I'd kiss you, and be able to say goodbye, and tell you how much I'll miss you and everyone, and maybe even be able to make you smile. And never feel we are apart, Mom. Because whenever you think of me, and you feel sad, just remember, God has let me be right there with you in your heart.'

"When I finished reading his letter, I was ashamed. I realized I was about to make a tragic mistake. I went back out to the garage, where I already had the car running with the garage doors closed. I threw open the big garage door and shut the car off. Then I went inside and read his letter over and over again.

"My boy, even at such a young age, had more common sense than me, I thought to myself. It was like he was right there beside me saying, 'Mom, why don't you do the beautiful things you always taught me to do. Carry on. Take it one day at a time. Keep going no matter what. And pray!'

"I kneeled down and cried. I thanked God for giving me such a fine and wonderful boy for those years I had him. I asked God's forgiveness for being so ungrateful. And I asked God to please take care of my boy now.

"When I look back on that horrible time when my son was killed and I almost took my own life, I realize the wonderful times with other children and grandchildren I would have missed, and the many lovely years of life I almost threw away. Now I realize that the darkest days of our lives only last a little while. Then the future arrives.

"Reading your book, Mr. Remick, after my eyes were washed clear with my own tears of sorrow, has given me the vision to see clearly and to understand why such wonderful, patriotic, God-fearing, young kids like my son want to volunteer to protect our country, even with all the potential risks to life involved."

While "Mary Kelly" was telling me her story, it washed her eyes clear with her own tears all over again. …. And it brought tears to mine. Just writing this, even now, makes my eyes gloss over. Her inspiring story reinforced my understanding of how important a tool the concept, TAKE ONE DAY AT A TIME, is for handling the worry and anxiety that come with a problem -- even the ultimate problem, the death of a loved one. I wanted to pass this story on to you as a poignant example of the second way to <u>HELP PEOPLE</u>.

We can never prepare for the worry and anxiety that everyone is bound to face some time in our lives over problems involving health, or taxes, or money, or jobs. We can never fully prepare for the trauma that a "Mary Kelly" or anyone else who loses a loved one, has to face. We cannot fully prepare for the kind of worry and anxiety that a young cadet Carl Morin felt either, or the stress that the thousands of others have felt on that first day of their four years at West Point. And when I say thousands of others, I'm not just talking about the young cadets -- the recent high school graduates; I'm also talking about their parents, and indeed, this applies to the parents of other kids leaving for other places. Parents can never fully prepare for the first time their kids leave home for the Service, or for the first time they deposit their kids far from home at any school or college.

Brigadier General Carl Morin had told me he would never forget that first day, "R-day," at West Point. Our son, Kyle, told us the same thing. For different reasons than theirs, Kyle's Mom and I shall never forget that day, either.

The first day at West Point, R-day, meaning Reception Day, is also the first day of Beast Barracks, the affectionate name for a high octane version of Army basic training. It is the rite of passage that must be met before being accepted into the Corps of Cadets and finally becoming a student when the academic year begins.

On our son's R-day, my wife and I empathetically felt his pain, and, knowing it was the beginning of an irrevocable change in our own lives, it left my wife in tears. But looking back now, I see it can also be a good example to give you of what will be our third way for you to <u>HELP PEOPLE</u> handle the worry and anxiety of a problem.

It's not as if we didn't try to prepare for that day. We knew that Kyle was one of about 1,400 accepted out of about 15,000 applicants who would have to find out if they could take the challenge of cadets their own age barking out orders at them; rousting them out of bed at 5 a.m. for a regimen of running, exercises, and marches in the rain lugging 50 pound rucksacks; constantly harassing and disciplining them; overloading them with Army knowledge; and at the end, marching them for fifteen miles under full pack.

We knew that Cadet Basic Training, in which much more testing, training, and knowledge than standard Army basic training is compressed into just 6 ½ weeks, was only the beginning of a high octane four years. It's not that we didn't know our son's being home for summer vacations would be a thing of the past because West Point wanted to cram as much knowledge and training as possible into him during those high octane four years. It's not that we didn't know we would talk to him very little on the phone, if at all, during those critical first several weeks, or not be able to see him for many weeks, or even months. It's not that we didn't know we were not just dropping off our son at a demanding college, but we were giving him over to our country. And, it's not that we didn't understand that, down the road at the end of this four-year West Point challenge, there could be some scary possibilities in store for him, and that meant for us, too. You would think we should have been prepared. But when the moment of truth -- saying goodbye -- actually came, it just hit us like a ton of bricks anyway.

Inside of a large auditorium sat the cadet candidates, and those who were with them, where a Lieutenant Colonel Lenz issued last minute instructions. When told to do so, the cadet candidates were to walk down the steps and onto the floor and line up, while those with them (who, for the most part, were parents) were to exit through the doors up above to the rear of the seats. The lieutenant colonel then turned the floor over to a sharp looking first-year (senior) cadet. Every one sat calmly listening to him say a few things. Then suddenly, like a bolt of lightning in a clear blue sky, he shocked everyone with:

"You now have ninety seconds to say goodbye!"

Ninety seconds? Only ninety seconds? Pandemonium broke out. Everyone was suddenly panic-stricken. Everyone rushed to hug and kiss and say everything in a hurry, all at once. What do you say in ninety seconds that accounts for eighteen years of life together? My mind raced backwards in time. As I watched my son hug his Mom during those precious seconds, eighteen years flashed by in my mind's eye. I saw my wife holding a newborn son, Kyle, in that hospital in Passaic, New Jersey; I saw a little boy neatly dressed in his official school uniform leaving for his very first day at the regular British school in Mildenhall, England; I saw the young baseball enthusiast practicing pitching on the mound and home plate he and I made together next to our driveway in Warren Grove, New Jersey; I saw the quarterback of his high school football team taking the hits as he threw the ball during his football games; I saw him laughing and posing with his Mom for pictures after his team won his final game in high school on Thanksgiving Day.

There was so much to say, and no time left. All I could weakly muster-up without my voice breaking up was, "Remember who you are, and where you came from, Kyle." His Mom just kept hugging him. Finally he said, "Well! I guess this is It!" He quietly walked down the steps. We quietly walked up the steps to exit out the back.

We turned and took one last look. So did he. For, it's not that we didn't know we would be seeing our boy for the last time -- he was about to be changed into a man, their man. I thought to myself, "Take a good look .... This is the last day -- these are the last seconds -- of our life with Kyle being completely with us and being completely ours." This was the first day of the rest of his life.

Through all the good times and hard times, we had somehow muddled through and managed to raise, certainly not gilded gold, but a fine and wholesome son who would be taking an oath later that day to defend our country. We had done our dead level best to take care of him during the eighteen years in the past. Now, we were leaving his future in the hands of God -- and West Point.

From that time forward, I decided that, because things were out of our hands and beyond our control, I had no choice but to cooperate with the inevitable. In order to live with the worry and anxiety, when all our tomorrows would start without our son, I resolved that I would mentally condition myself to accept what fate had to offer. What will be, will be. I would always hope and pray for the best, but, in the back of my mind, I would be prepared for the worst. And that's the third way I am telling you to HELP PEOPLE. That's the third way to help those you lead to handle the worries and anxieties that accompany a problem. Teach them to:

3.) – PREPARE TO ACCEPT THE WORST

Am I saying that your people should roll over and play dead every time they are confronted with a problem? Of course not. Tell them, as long as there is a chance to prevent the worst from happening, fight like hell! What I'm saying is, tell them that before the worst has happened, think of what is the worst that can happen, accept that it may happen, and then try to improve on the worst as much as they can. But, on the other hand, if they are up against something that they cannot possibly alter -- if something is what it is, and cannot be otherwise -- then, accept the inevitable. Tell them it does no one any good if they worry themselves to death over it.

Ronald Reagan, "The Gipper," was an awe-inspiring example of someone who knew how to PREPARE TO ACCEPT THE WORST and knew how to accept what might be the inevitable. Going back to that chilly, overcast, shocking day in March of 1981 when he lay close to death with an assassin's bullet through his lung, lodged one inch from his heart, and going in and out of consciousness, he prepared for the worst and what might be the inevitable. How do I know? I know because, he prayed. That comes from -- this all comes from -- a person at the hospital who was there at the time.

As he lay there semi-conscious on the gurney close to death before going into the operating room, completely naked with only a sheet over him, he was aware that the hand of a kindly (unnamed) female was holding his hand to comfort him. Knowing his wife, Nancy, wasn't there, he asked, "Who's holding my hand?" No one answered. He went unconscious again. When he came back to being semi-conscious and he felt his hand still being held, he opened his eyes and said, "Does Nancy know about this?"

As he was being wheeled into the operating room, hearing people around him sobbing over him, he said to them, "Don't worry, wait here, I'll be right back." Though still semi-conscious, yet preparing for the worst, knowing this operation would put enormous stresses and worries on the doctors and nurses, he tried to relieve the stresses by saying to one of them something like, "I only hope you're a Republican." One of the doctors replied, "Today Mr. President, we are all Republicans."

After the operation, in the recovery room, still not out of the woods, still in critical condition, and still too close for comfort to "changing worlds," he opened his eyes and looked up to see his wife Nancy. Seeing the worry and pain on her face, he showed her he had made peace with his Maker and was himself free of worry and anxiety by weakly but playfully saying to her, "Honey, I forgot to duck." Even when in the fight of his life, Ronald Reagan had the character and inner strength to PREPARE TO ACCEPT THE WORST, and was prepared for the inevitable.

Now, someone you are the leader of might say, "I can prepare to accept the worst, but if the worst does happen, or has already happened, then what do I do?"

That's a fair question. You can answer them this way. Tell them:

"You've heard the timeworn proverb, 'Don't cry over spilled milk." And, you've heard, 'All the king's horses and all the king's men cannot put what's broken back together again.' Maybe you've heard, 'Sanity, like glass and china, is easily shattered, and never well mended.' And perhaps you've heard,

'Worry, like drink, does not drown a problem, but waters it, and makes it grow faster.' Those timeworn proverbs are timeworn because they've been time-tested and found to be accurate and predictive. They're a part of the distilled wisdom of civilization that has been shaped and tempered in the fiery furnaces of experience and handed down to us through the centuries. So, when the worst has already happened, and what's done is done and cannot be otherwise, you should -- after according the problem the appropriate respect -- go on to also accord those proverbs and the wisdom of the ages your appropriate respect and accept your 'fait accompli.' But that's not all. Then you <u>must</u> assume a positive attitude, and do what the following well-known bit of folk wisdom advises: 'When you have a lemon, make a lemonade'."

You get the idea, right? In a nutshell, tell them they must go forward and do the next best thing.

As I mentally march across the decades of my memory to write this book, how I wish I had been smart enough to take advice like that, and use it, all my life. Why didn't I? I don't know. But I finally smartened up. And thank Heavens I did! For, what a saving grace it was. What a colossal difference it made once upon a time in my life. It was probably the bitterest moment in my life. It was a time of crisis, when all of my plans and dreams and life's work thus far came a hair's breadth away from going up in smoke, taking my mission and career with it. It's a mind-blowing story. Here it is.

It all began when we, for what I later considered to be bittersweet reasons, pulled up roots and went to England to set up a company, which became Packages For Semiconductors -- the one I talked about earlier in this book. Bittersweet? Yes. The sweet part is because some one must have had an awful lot of confidence that I had the right stuff to pull this thing off. Bitter? Yes. Bitter because of the surreptitious ways and reasons it was all made to come about. But that's another story, perhaps for another day.

I was so earnest about this challenge, I spent months methodically doing all the right things that an entrepreneur needs to do to start a new company. I secured a factory through the British Ministry of Trade and Industry, rent-free for two years in Cwmbrn, Monmouthshire, and a council house to live in. I sold our house in New Jersey and everything we had to our name to raise money to purchase my manufacturing equipment and direct materials, and to pay deposits for riggers, truckers, plumbers, electricians, utilities, and the supply of indirect materials and services for setting up and operating the company.

All we had then were the shirts on our backs and the rest of our clothes and household goods packed in several trunks for shipping. I arranged to have riggers and truckers deliver my manufacturing equipment and the trunks to a container in Port Newark for transport by ship to London. We were ready to go. There was a going-away party for us by our friends. We said our goodbyes all around. Then, finally, after months of planning, my wife and eighteen months old son and I boarded a British Airways Boeing 747 at Kennedy Airport in New York for the flight to London.

I had reservations at the reasonably priced Royal Bayswater Hotel across Bayswater Road from Hyde Park in London for close access to the Pork of London for our clothing and personal goods, and for arranging to have my equipment shipped to a factory.

The day after we arrived, trade union strikes broke out all over London. They shut off the flow at British Gas, so there was no heat in our hotel or at any of the London hotels during the middle of February, the coldest month. On top of that, we couldn't get our clothes because the dockworkers had joined the strikes.

Meanwhile, I took the two-hour train ride from London to Monmouthshire to get the keys and, being all charged up, have a look at our factory and house. When I arrived, an official and an MI-5 officer sat down with me and told me they had given the factory and house to someone else! "What?" I said, "After months of transatlantic telephone calls, and several letters confirming everything, and completely pulling up roots in the USA, and traveling all the way to Britain with a wife and eighteen month old baby in tow, and all of our equipment, clothes, and personal goods having hit the docks of London, you have the audacity to tell me this, <u>now</u>?" "Why", I asked, "would you do such a thing?" No answer. "Is it because I'm American?" They said, no. "Then why?" Their answer was -- and I remember the exact words, as if it were today -- their answer was, "We just don't want your kind here." I couldn't have been more stunned if they had punched me in the face. I was staggered.

That night back at the hotel in London, I told my wife all about it, but I also told her I had already arranged to meet with the Monmouthshire member of the House of Lords, Lord Ragland, and with the US Embassy in London. Maybe there was still hope.

I got no joy with the Lord Ragland idea, and, after the US Embassy checked with someone in Washington, they told me it would be "unwise" for them to help me. They went on to tell me that I would have to "soldier on" and make it work on my own.

I got back to the hotel and told my wife. That was the last straw. She was distraught. We were all alone in a foreign country with no place to live; we were sleeping in our clothes and overcoats because of there being no heat; we were washing our underwear in the bathroom sink because we could not get our clothes from the London dockyards -- all of this with a little 18-month-old boy. I had to wonder how much longer she could hold it all in. It was enough to make anyone break down and cry. And she did.

The worst had happened, I thought. Everything was going wrong, and through no fault of my own. I knew I was at one of those crossroads of life. Which way should I go? What should I do? I had to make what would be a monumental decision in my life. Should I defy my commitments and obligations? Could I? I did have good reason to. I was beside myself over the turn of events. My insides were twisting and turning and burning. The thought of potential near-term poverty began to haunt me day and night. I was so upset, I had a hard time sleeping. When I tried to sleep, the decision I had to make kept my heart awake.

I thought about it long and hard. I knew that we shouldn't cry over milk already spilled down the drain. This was more than milk, however. A lot of money was already spilled down the drain. On the other hand, with all of the sweat, and now the tears, at least no blood had been spilled -- yet. My wife and son still had their health. I still had my health and my education and my experience. Although it seemed like the worst had happened, was it really the worst?

Suddenly, something dawned on me. A little light lit up in my head. I remembered these words my mother always used to say to us, "When the worst happens, or you don't get what your heart desires, do the next best thing." I remember her saying those words many times, but this time they really, really registered with me. "Right", I said to myself. "You've absolutely hit bottom, so there's nowhere to go but up." When I told my wife that, she agreed with me. And, after having relieved all of her worry and anxiety and dismay with that good cry she had, she told me she'd be right there with me when I went on and did the next best thing.

As little strokes fell great oaks, little by little we retooled our lives in England. The labor strikes finally ended. I made arrangements to stay at the Royal Bayswater Hotel at a reduced monthly rate. We bought some new clothes to supplement those we had. And, after two months, I finally secured another factory and council house in a new development area two hours north of London in East Anglia, to which we moved.

We finally got the equipment and our trunks. As a precaution, we not only lived out of our trunks, but off of our trunks -- trunks as our chairs and tables and everything else except beds -- until I was sure the company was off the ground, and we knew we would be there for a while. In fact, even when we finally got some real furniture, bidding for it at auctions, we decided to live a Spartan lifestyle, like most council house residents and our son's little British friends did, until our firm was a bona fide, running, successful enterprise.

So, we know all about hitting bottom. When the worst happens, we know it doesn't kill you. And when the well runs dry, you begin to appreciate the worth of water. I'm almost glad we had that traumatic mind-blowing experience because now, whenever the worst happens, and worry and anxiety weigh heavy on us and threaten to spoil our lives, I always remember that time when we lived out of and off of our trunks; when we hit bottom and had nowhere to go but up; and when we were alone in our new world and, at one point, didn't have a dime -- but we had each other. I call it "the hungry years." In many ways, they were the best years of our lives. I miss the hungry years.

Am I happy I made that decision long ago not to lament what could not be changed, but instead, decided to do the next best thing and start again? Can I truly say I never regretted that decision during, or since, the eighteen years we ended up having our company in England? It's true, during the early years we did know worry and anxiety and struggle and despair. We knew what it was like to be on the battlefield of ups and downs, victories and defeats, shattered dreams and broken promises, life and death; always fighting on that battlefield with the odds stacked against my mission. Yet, you will see me shed no tears over it, nor envy those who have had it easier than I on the way to being successful. When we meet our Maker, and He looks at our life, I know His records will show that we have lived real life and have done something special. And He will know that the School of Hard Knocks made us know things and see things and live a philosophy of life that most would never know or see or live. That School has taught me not to dread problems. And it has insulated me from letting little trivialities bother me. For, when you have survived after everything has suddenly come crashing down on your head, it somehow doesn't matter much again whether you use the correct fork to eat your salad. It has taught me not to expect too much from people. It has taught me not to let criticism bother me. I have learned to count my blessings. I have learned that there are not only spiritual, but also practical benefits to prayer. I understand what is meant when they say: "There are no atheists in foxholes."

So, do I regret all the hardship? <u>Absolutely not</u>. I more and more deeply appreciate what God has given us on this good

Earth of His. When we come to the end of life and can't take our worldly treasures with us and can only take ourselves, then character will be the only treasure we can offer in order to get where we want to go. And that will be worth the price we had to pay.

How did it all end for me? Well, let me put it straight and simple. The Berlin Wall came down. The Cold War ended. My mission ended. I came home -- to stay.

That's what happened to us, once upon a time in England. That's the true story of how we were once upon a time crushed, but in the end, survived that most bleak and desperate time of our lives, guided by the techniques I give you in this chapter to HELP PEOPLE handle the worry and anxiety that come with problems. And, in particular, one of these techniques is based on the following simple words of wisdom that my mother always used to tell us:

4.) – DO THE NEXT BEST THING

Now I've told you those simple words of wisdom, too. And that's the fourth way for you, as a great real-life leader to HELP PEOPLE.

We're often told, "crisis is the mother of invention." I can attest to the truth of that, and can talk from experience about the subject, as someone who has been lucky enough to successfully turn lemons into lemonade. But, amazing to me, the more history and biographies I read, and the more I see how "John" and "Jenny" react under terrible circumstances, the more heartened I am by the way my fellow human beings, in general, have had the wonder-filled ability to handle worry, anxiety, tragedy, death, -- and then go forward to DO THE NEXT BEST THING.

Beethoven had a bright future ahead of him -- until he began to go deaf. Did he collapse from worry and anxiety over it? No. When he went deaf, he was determined to DO THE NEXT

BEST THING. Like you can "see" an event in your mind's eye, he "heard" his music in his mind's ear. That's what actually made his music unique. Perhaps, if Beethoven had not gone deaf, he would not have reached his pinnacle of greatness in the world of classical music.

Ray Charles and Stevie Wonder did the same thing in modern times. They were both blind, but did they give up? No. They both did the next best thing. They worked out a way to write modern music and sing their tunes themselves.

Reginald Carey Harrison was a trim, handsome, 6'-1" tall young man with outstanding athletic ability. He would have been popular with everyone, especially the girls, as a footballer, "rugger," or cricketer, but he went blind in one eye after a childhood illness. Having difficulty doing sports with the use of only one eye, but still aspiring to fame (and to popularity with the girls), he decided to DO THE NEXT BEST THING. He signed up for drama classes to try his hand at acting. Yes, Reginald Carey Harrison -- better known as Rex Harrison -- was launched on his brilliant acting career by doing the next best thing because of his little secret: he was blind in one eye from a youthful disease. The rest of the story is movie history.

And how about our eighteenth president of the United States and final Union Army commanding general in the Civil War who was the one that was able to finally defeat the Confederate Army's incredible General Robert E. Lee. Yes, I'm talking about Ulysses S. Grant, again.

After graduating from West Point, he served several years in the Army. He then left the Army to follow his dream of becoming a big man in business and commerce. But, one venture after another failed. What did Ulysses S. Grant do? He decided to DO THE NEXT BEST THING. He went back to the Army. The day he again donned the uniform, lady luck must have been smiling at Abraham Lincoln. Grant led the Union

Army on to victory for Lincoln. He was, a few years later, rewarded by being elected President of the United States.

There was once a young man in London who, although having had only half a dozen years of schooling, dreamed of being a writer of stories. Why only half a dozen years schooling? Because, at a very young age, he was forced to go to work when his father was thrown into Marshalsea Debtors' Prison. He was sent to work at a shoe-blacking factory in the slums of London where child labor was rampant. That miserable experience psychologically scarred him for life and haunted him all the rest of his days. At all costs, he wanted out of there, never to return.

Story after story written by our aspiring young writer was refused by editors. Finally, one day, he decided to DO THE NEXT BEST THING. He offered to just give an editor one of his stories without being paid for it, if the editor would give it a chance and print it. The editor agreed. It was printed, and it was well received. That day, our young man wandered all around London, avoiding everyone, because he did not want them to see the tears of joy that he could not hold back.

Getting that first story in print completely changed the young man's life. He went on to write quite a few other stories and books that were well received. And, he was well paid for them. He could say goodbye forever to shame, and hunger, and squalor, and the factories of London, and sleeping in dark and dirty rooms. He no longer had to rub elbows with streetfulls of rogues, whores, thieves, and vagrants, sodomites, pickpockets, and other filth and cutthroats and gutter-snipes of London – except in the future books he wrote -- like *David Copperfield*. Have you guessed who this young man was? You may have heard of him. His name was Charles Dickens.

Can you guess what Lord Byron, Percy Shelley, Rudyard Kipling, Henry Thoreau, Walt Whitman, Leo Tolstoy, Nathaniel Hawthorne, Alfred Lord Tennyson, and West Pointer Edgar Allan Poe all had in common? If you say that they were all men, you're right. But, once again, that's not the answer I'm looking for. If you say they were all authors, again you are correct. But that's not the answer I'm looking for, either. Then what is it? They were all men who, at one point in time, could not get their writings published or printed. They were all authors who, therefore, decided to DO THE NEXT BEST THING. They arranged on their own to publish or print their own work. What a loss it would have been to the world if these legendary authors had decided to give up rather than DO THE NEXT BEST THING.

By now, the next logical question has perhaps occurred to you. If not, please allow me to put words in your mouth. "When the worst has already happened, and I decide to DO THE NEXT BEST THING, how do I know <u>what</u> the next best thing is?" Well, here is how you do that.

Thus far I have given you four ways to <u>HELP PEOPLE</u> by teaching them how to handle the worry and anxiety that accompanies a problem. We have not talked about helping them to solve the actual problem itself however, in the case of a problem that <u>can</u> be solved, or to pinpoint <u>what</u> is the next best thing to do in the case of a problem that <u>cannot</u> be solved. That's what we'll do now to round out <u>KEY # 5: HELP PEOPLE</u>. We'll begin simply, with a quick and easy and surefire approach that never fails:

5.) – HAVE ALL THE FACTS AND INFORMATION

To illustrate, here's an example of that surefire approach which I first learned from personal experience years ago when I was a senior in high school and the quarterback of our football team. During the pre-season, my coach pulled me aside and laid down the law. He told me I had to learn what every position on the team does on every play in our playbook. Although our core play sequence was an option type of offense, overall we were a multiple offense running our plays from the T-formation and from the shotgun, and even from the old single wing. Therefore, our playbook had one hundred plays!

Half balking at the load laid on me and half really wanting to know why, I asked the coach, "Why do I have to know what everybody's assignment is?" He said: "If you want to be my quarterback, just do it. You'll find out why." So, I did it. It turned out to be easier than I thought it would be. .... A lot of redundancy was involved.

As the season progressed, I began to see what my coach meant by, "You'll find out why." It got to the point that on practically every other play that I called in the huddle, some one or other would have a problem and, slightly panicky, whisper to me, "Hey Rem., whad-oo I do on that play?" And, I could actually tell them! Very quickly I noticed that a lot of the guys began to depend on me to help them. Although a more popular guy was made the team captain, I automatically became the team's actual leader because they knew when they came to me, I could bail them out of their problem, quickly and easily. Even the team captain came to me during games.

The point of this story, and the simple concept I want to get across to you with it is: When you HAVE ALL THE FACTS AND INFORMATION, often times you can <u>HELP PEOPLE</u> by simply <u>telling them</u> the answer or the solution.

Does that simple approach work in all walks of life? You bet it does. I can give you bunches of examples of people and stories like the one I just told you. But I think you get it without my having to do that. There is no way that you and I, or Plato and Einstein, or super-fast cryogenically-cooled computers can be wired brilliantly enough to arrive at valid solutions and decisions to <u>any</u> problem without first having all the facts and information. It's no big secret or mystery. You don't have to study at Princeton for four years to understand how important it is to HAVE ALL THE FACTS AND INFORMATION in order to honestly and legitimately <u>HELP PEOPLE</u>.

So in some circumstances, like the one I gave you, it's easy to HELP PEOPLE to solve their problem by simply telling them the answer. However, in many circumstances, the problem doesn't lend itself to such an easy fix. Many problems are more complicated and challenging. But let not your heart be troubled. I'm now going to tell you how you can help your people and be their hero in the most difficult circumstances, also. Does this sound like you're about to get a sermon from the *Bible*? Okay then. I won't proselytize. But, as even the *Bible* is a book of stories and examples, and the best sermon is a good example, let me give you a good non-Biblical example, using someone you learned about in history.

When still a young man in his twenties, Franklin, already had the wit and wisdom and ambition and love of country to be a rising star in America. Being well connected in his State, and having his heart in the right place, he was popular enough to be elected to office in the state legislature and appointed to important positions. Then, little known to people nowadays, at the age of thirty-four on a trip to Canada, he was afflicted with a devastating and debilitating kind of paralysis. It was just about the worst that could happen (if you leave out death). The doctors told him he would be crippled from the waist down and that he would never regain the use of his legs. What he had, later came to be known as polio. Did you know that Franklin was crippled from the waist down?

He dropped out of public view and public life for quite some time, but not because he had given up. He did not give up. He was determined to fight like heck to disprove the doctors and try to beat this thing by following an exhaustive regimen of swimming and other exercises. He did this faithfully for month after month, but nothing worked for him. The doctors were right after all.

Finally he conceded, and accepted the worst -- he was crippled for life and would never have use of his legs again. That's when he became determined to DO THE NEXT BEST THING. And, to figure out what the next best thing was, he began reading anything and everything available at the time in order to HAVE

ALL THE FACTS AND INFORMATION at his fingertips. After digesting and analyzing all the facts, he worked out a way, when fitted-up with special braces on his legs and his hips, to "walk" a short distance by swiveling his torso. Then he would casually hold-on to something or someone next to him while standing in front of an audience making a speech, for instance. He hated and avoided the wheelchair.

Franklin went from strength to strength, confidence to more confidence, and finally he was ready to re-emerge to try getting back to his career in government. And, wow, did he indeed get back to his career! First he got himself elected governor of the state. Then, four years later, he was elected President of the United States! What? That's right. President. Our Franklin is not Benjamin Franklin, if that's what you've been thinking. Our Franklin is Franklin Delano Roosevelt (FDR), our 32nd President, and the only one, ever, elected President four times (1932, 1936, 1940, 1944). No one else was even elected three times. And, do you know why FDR's image is on our ten cent coin, our dime? It's because he was the prime mover behind the give-a-dime drive that provided money for the research that ultimately led to a cure for polio. They called it "The March of Dimes." Wouldn't you say America is lucky that Franklin didn't give up, but decided to HAVE ALL THE FACTS AND INFORMATION at his disposal so he could DO THE NEXT BEST THING? I would.

FDR went from being a dejected and hopeless cripple to being the most powerful man on the face of the earth. It almost sounds like he must have used some kind of secret magic or wizardry to deal with the problem, doesn't it? Well, he did. But, as we know, like all secret magic and wizardry, it isn't that secret or magical or mystical or difficult or complicated once someone shows you how to do it. Shall I show you? Okay. Here we go then. We'll take FDR as an example again.

When he finally conceded that he had a crippling disease, and it could never be different, and he decided to DO THE NEXT BEST THING, it was then that his next problem automatically reared its head. That problem was: What is the next best thing?

That's when he put his nose to the grindstone and sifted through everything he could lay his hands on in order to HAVE ALL THE FACTS AND INFORMATIOIN at his fingertips so he could go on and employ the magic of the "problem wizard", which is:

First – Understand exactly what the problem is:

(In FDR's case, the problem was that he wanted to get back to his career in public life, but he didn't have the "wheels" to get around on his own.)

Second – Identify what the cause of the problem is:

(That was easy. He had no use of his legs because he had polio for which there was no cure; and therefore, he could not campaign or win looking like a helpless cripple.)

Third – Find what the potential solutions are:

(His options were: give it up; use a wheelchair; have handlers and a dolly-on-wheels move him around; try to have special braces hidden under his clothes and train himself to shuffle under his own steam at least several steps without toppling over.)

Fourth – Decide what the best solution is:

(FDR decided to work with the possibility of special braces so he could appear "normal" to the electorate.

FDR's solution to the problem of finding what was the next best thing -- the braces -- using the "problem wizard" type of reasoning worked for him for over seventeen years as a Governor and as the President of the United States.

The "problem wizard" type of reasoning has worked its wonders for hundreds of years for people from Plato and Aristotle, to Newton and Edison, and for thousands upon thousands of others, including me. I have used it throughout my adult life to solve all kinds of problems from business decisions, to engineering analysis, to manufacturing problem solving, to making groundbreaking historical research discoveries. So, to HELP PEOPLE solve their actual problem, as opposed to the problem of worry and anxiety over the actual problem, do as FDR did:

6.) – EMPLOY THE "PROBLEM WIZARD":

First – UNDERSTAND EXACTLY WHAT THE PROBLEM IS.
Second – IDENTIFY WHAT THE CAUSE OF THE PROBLEM IS.
Third – FIND WHAT THE POTENTIAL SOLUTIONS ARE.
Fourth – DECIDE WHAT THE BEST SOLUTION IS.

So there you have it. Unusual for a book on leadership, I have devoted an entire chapter to worry and anxiety and problem solving to help make you a great real-life leader. Again, here's how it does that. When you HELP PEOPLE to handle the potentially devastating worry and anxiety of a problem that could have resulted in tragedy for them in their lives, you will forge an everlasting personal bond with them (and a great reputation with others who know what you did). They will become beholden to you forever. For you may have saved their sanity or their lives. You will be not only their leader, but their hero. You will become something that is very rare: a leader who is loved!
    That's why our KEY # 5: HELP PEOPLE, and this unusual chapter for a book on leadership is incredibly important. It keeps you squarely on track for rising to the top of the heap as a great real-life leader of character. Franklin D. Roosevelt knew that, way back in his time. Now you know it, too.

Here is a divine little piece of philosophical wisdom, written by Dr. Reinbold Niebuhr, that puts the underlying philosophy of this entire chapter in a nutshell.

"God grant me:

The serenity to accept the things I cannot change;
(handle worry and anxiety)

The courage to change the things I can;
(use the "problem wizard")

And the wisdom to know the difference."

You can start to help people by getting them to digest that piece of wisdom first. And, before I end this chapter, I would like to direct a bit of wisdom about worry and anxiety that I mentioned earlier in the chapter right straight at you, the leader, this time. Do you remember when I said, "Funerals and hospital beds come at an expensive price -- and come suddenly -- in this day and age?" Well, before you preach to someone else, remember those ringing words of MacArthur at West Point, "Master yourself before you seek to master others." Was MacArthur also speaking to you? Perhaps. Think about it.

Okay, then. Let's get down to the practical business of helping your people, and perhaps yourself, by employing:

KEY # 5: HELP PEOPLE

And let's implement KEY # 5 by teaching people how to:

1.) – KEEP BUSY.

2.) – TAKE ONE DAY AT A TIME.

3.) – PREPARE TO ACCEPT THE WORST.

4.) – DO THE NEXT BEST THING.

5.) – HAVE ALL THE FACTS AND INFORMATION.

6.) – EMPLOY THE "PROBLEM WIZARD."

******************* *PART III* *******************

TAKE CARE OF DOING IT WELL
*

Chapter 7: Implementing What You Have Learned

Have you thought about MacArthur's: "Master yourself before you seek to master others?" I don't mean to say that you or I or Mother Theresa or the Supreme Court can ever be perfect at implementing our FIVE KEYS to great real-life leadership, which, in summary are:

KEY # 1: BEGIN BY GETTING PEOPLE ON YOUR SIDE.

KEY # 2: CORRECT PEOPLE WITHOUT CONDEMNING OR CRITICIZING

KEY # 3: MAKE PEOPLE FEEL IMPORTANT.

KEY # 4: AROUSE PRIDE AND THE EMOTIONS.

KEY # 5: HELP PEOPLE.

You'll find that the best thing about these KEYS is that they're practical and easy to work with. You don't have to be perfect to make them work. No one is perfect. If you and I were perfect, you wouldn't be reading this book and I wouldn't have time to write it. You or I would be sitting in the White House as the wisest President that the United States ever had, or we'd be working on Wall Street pulling in more money than any human being has a right to have.

I'll never forget what happened on a cold winter night years ago in New York City during the days when I was still a bachelor,

150

and had not yet met my future wife. I was in a singles club on the Upper East Side of Manhattan with a friend from Toronto, Ontario, Canada whose name is Ed Hradowy. By 11 pm on that Friday evening, feeling a bit happy, Ed was unwelcomingly trying to chat-up this attractive young lady who was sitting at the bar listening to the music with her girlfriend. He was trying, in vain, to get her to give him her name and telephone number, saying, "Maybe we can have dinner together, and, who knows? What do you think?" Hearing that, she finally turned to him saying, "And what did you say your name is?" That sounded like progress to Ed, so with as little modesty imaginable, in his best James Bond impersonation, he said, "Hradowy is the name - - Ed Hradowy." With that, she swung the cold shoulder she had been giving him right around, looked him straight in the face, and said, "Well, Ed, guess what! I think you're a perfect ass." She gave him the cold shoulder again, turning around. I almost sprayed the beer out of my mouth all over Ed with laughter. Never one to be left speechless, Ed leaned way over the bar, looked her straight in the face in return, and, with his unique, gravelly, slight Canadian accent, responded to her by saying, "My dear …… nothing is perfect!" I burst into laughter again. So did the girlfriend. Ed just smiled a satisfying smile. As we started to leave for more salubrious climes of the bar, the object of Ed's affections turned around again, and, this time attractively kind of chuckling and reaching out her hand, said, "Okay, Ed Thataway or Whichaway or whatever you said your name is, we're even …… my name is Kathy." They hit it off real well from that point on.

Whenever I want to make the point: Nothing is perfect, and no one is perfect, but you don't have to be perfect to get results, I always think of that classic encounter of boy meets girl.

So, when you begin to implement the FIVE KEYS, if it's not all perfect the first time, don't be discouraged. Go back and review the book. Review the parts that apply to what you're doing. Underline those parts. Study them. Think about them. Make notes on the pages that I have provided at the end of this book for that purpose. Then apply them again to what you're doing. It's not unusual to have to do that. I spent almost ten years on my book, *West Point ... Thomas Jefferson*, and I find I have to keep looking it over again from time to time to jog my own memory about things I wrote in my own book. So, don't worry! When it comes to worry and anxiety, you now know how to "master yourself before you seek to master others." Try again.

Do you remember what I told you at the beginning of the book? This book is not merely for reading on the beach. This is a book for doing. It's a book from which you are forming new habits and a new way of life. It's a guidebook and working manual for becoming a great real-life leader of character.

And remember, great real-life leaders of character are not just folks who are in charge. They are people who have the ability to get things
done, and get them done well by getting people to <u>want</u> to cooperate, and <u>want</u> to do the very best they can do, <u>willingly and voluntarily</u>.

And remember, if you just take what I have told you here, not only into your mind and into your memory, but into your heart and soul, you will have a new glow and charisma that others have never seen in you before, but will now see. You will begin to soar like an eagle above the ordinary, boring, pedestrian, self-centered leaders who think everyone should fall all over themselves to please <u>them</u>.

And remember, though this book will work magic for you, like all magic, you have to know how to do it, and practice it. Only then will you be able to put the powers you possess to good use, and bring about a virtual sea change in the cooperation of your people with you.

And remember, when you are using the FIVE KEYS, use them like you are a one-man "team" -- a combination of <u>t</u>eacher, <u>e</u>vangelist, <u>and</u> <u>m</u>issionary, all of whom, teach. "Teams" are not necessarily great leaders, but great leaders are necessarily "teams". Teachers are not necessarily great leaders, but great leaders are necessarily teachers. If you teach them, they will follow.

And remember, when you are teaching, do it with a positive attitude and enthusiasm. Look people straight in the eye, and keep looking them straight in the eye as you speak to them. Eye-to-eye contact actually exhibits a little bit of its own magic, in addition to the magic you can accomplish by using what you have learned in this book.

And remember, if you work hard toward your goal with a burning desire and dogged determination that comes from your heart, you can achieve wonders. When you become a great real-life leader it will be the touchstone of your career, and indeed, of your whole life.

And remember what Thomas Jefferson said: "Youth is a time when great exertions are necessary but you have little time left to make them." If you put the keys and techniques in this book to work immediately, you can count on this: One fine day a few years from now, you will wake up in the morning and find that your exertions have made you one of the great real-life leaders in America.

And remember these words of mine: "Someone reading this book may someday become the President of the United States or even be one of the greatest leaders of all time. When I finally "cross the river", I want you to know that I will go there proudly knowing I helped to make it happen and I will go there proudly saying, as Rudyard Kipling said about Gunga Din, "You're a better man than I.""

<u>Acknowledgment</u>

I would like to express my love, gratitude, and appreciation to my dear wife Diane who, once again, during the long odyssey of my writing this book, exhibited the patience of an angel and the unselfishness of a saint during the many thousands of hours that I was "away" in another room, buried in thought.

*

I also wish to thank my editor, Myra Olshansky, for her kindness and gentleness and expertise and timely attention to my manuscript.

Also by
NORMAN THOMAS REMICK

Mr. Jefferson's Academy: The Real Story
ISBN 0967487900
&
Understanding West Point, Leaders of Character, and Thomas Jefferson
ISBN 0967487919 = 9780967487915

Notes

156

Notes

Notes

158

Notes

Notes